Advance praise for *A Tale of Two Quagmir*

MW01049226

"The plethora of best-selling new books on tactical errors and leaves the false impression that had the war been fought differently, victory would have been achieved and U.S. interests advanced. Campbell's lucidly written comparison of the wars in Vietnam and Iraq shows how costly this illusion is, a deception consciously fostered by American leaders and cheerleading members of the Fourth Estate." —**Lieutenant General William E. Odom (U.S. Army, retired),** senior fellow with the Hudson Institute and former director of the National Security Agency during the Reagan Administration

"Campbell cuts through the rhetoric and obfuscation that passes for debate over Vietnam and Iraq, offering in their place measured, thoughtful, clear-sighted analysis. Anyone who wants to understand two of the greatest debacles of my generation, how they relate to each other, and what we might do to avoid future such failures needs to read this book." —**W. D. Ehrhart,** author of *Vietnam Perkasie: A Combat Marine Memoir*

"*A Tale of Two Quagmires* is a passionate and thoughtful analysis of the old war in Vietnam and the new one in Iraq. Kenneth Campbell understands war as a veteran and as an historian. The book is an invaluable aid to understanding the past and the present." —**Marilyn B. Young,** New York University, author of *The Vietnam Wars, 1945-1990*

"*A Tale of Two Quagmires* is a concise, cogent, meticulously researched examination of how the American public was deliberately misled into ruinous military adventures in Vietnam and Iraq and of the 'crucial lessons' that must be acknowledged in order to avoid such debacles in the future. Once a young, battle-hardened Marine determined to survive his time in a war of dubious necessity, now a highly regarded scholar of international affairs, Professor Ken Campbell offers a reasoned alternative to this cycle of deception and quagmire. In doing so he does not entirely reject the necessity of wars: only those without legitimate purpose and clear-cut strategy. The wisdom contained in *A Tale of Two Quagmires* has the potential to put the United States on a road to re-capturing 'the moral high ground in international relations' and, in the process, spare humanity the horrific consequences of such senseless and protracted conflicts—a gift beyond value to future generations." —**Michael Archer,** author of *A Patch of Ground: Khe Sanh Remembered*

"Informed by the hard lessons of first-hand experience and a lifetime of reflection, Ken Campbell offers a compelling and heart-wrenching story of America at war. Whether liberal or conservative, hawkish or dovish, thoughtful citizens must confront the questions Campbell bravely raises. America's aspirations as a moral nation depend on voices like Ken Campbell's—voices that challenge conventional wisdom, generate debate, and put into motion the forces of self-correction that keep us true to the best of our values and traditions." —**Joel H. Rosenthal,** president, Carnegie Council for Ethics in International Affairs

A Tale of Two Quagmires

The Invasion of Grenada

I didn't want a monument,
not even one as sober as that
vast black wall of broken lives.
I didn't want a postage stamp.
I didn't want a road beside the Delaware
River with a sign proclaiming:
"Vietnam Veterans Memorial Highway."

What I wanted was a simple recognition
of the limits of our power as a nation
to inflict our will on others.
What I wanted was an understanding
that the world is neither black-and-white
nor ours.

What I wanted
was an end to monuments.

—*W. D. Ehrhart*

A Tale of Two Quagmires

Iraq, Vietnam, and the Hard Lessons of War

Kenneth J. Campbell
University of Delaware

Foreword by Richard Falk

Paradigm Publishers
Boulder • London

INITIATIVE

Paradigm Publishers is committed to preserving ancient forests and natural resources. We elected to print *A Tale Of Two Quagmires* on 30% post consumer recycled paper, processed chlorine free. As a result, for this printing, we have saved:

8 Trees (40' tall and 6-8" diameter)
3,555 Gallons of Wastewater
1,430 Kilowatt Hours of Electricity
392 Pounds of Solid Waste
770 Pounds of Greenhouse Gases

Paradigm Publishers made this paper choice because our printer, Thomson-Shore, Inc., is a member of Green Press Initiative, a nonprofit program dedicated to supporting authors, publishers, and suppliers in their efforts to reduce their use of fiber obtained from endangered forests.

For more information, visit www.greenpressinitiative.org

"The Invasion of Grenada" is reprinted from *Carrying the Darkness: The Poetry of the Vietnam War*, W. D. Ehrhart, ed. (Lubbock: Texas Tech University Press, 1989). Reprinted by permission of the author.

Copyright © 2007 Paradigm Publishers

Published in the United States by Paradigm Publishers, 3360 Mitchell Lane, Suite E, Boulder, CO 80301 USA.

Paradigm Publishers is the trade name of Birkenkamp & Company, LLC,
Dean Birkenkamp, President and Publisher.

Library of Congress Cataloging-in-Publication Data

A tale of two quagmires : Iraq, Vietnam, and the hard lessons of war / Kenneth J. Campbell.
        p. cm.—(International studies intensives)
Includes bibliographical references and index.
ISBN-13: 978-1-59451-351-0 (hc)
ISBN-10: 1-59451-351-1 (hc)
ISBN-13: 978-1-59451-352-7 (pb)
ISBN-10: 1-59451-352-X (pb)
1. Iraq War, 2003- 2. Vietnam War, 1961-1975. I. Campbell, Kenneth J.
DS79.76.A875 2007
956.7044'3—dc22

                                                                              2006037219

Printed and bound in the United States of America on acid-free paper that meets the standards of the American National Standard for Permanence of Paper for Printed Library Materials.

Designed and Typeset by Straight Creek Bookmakers.

11 10 09 08 07 1 2 3 4 5

To my daughter, Meagan, and my nephews and nieces, Keith, Christopher, Stephen, Shannon, Geoffrey, Mandi, Andrew, Jessica, Justin, Taylor, Anthony, and Theresa.

CONTENTS

FOREWORD

Almost thirty-five years ago three young Americans recently returned from the killing fields of Vietnam told their stories of the war in the living room of my Princeton home. They repeatedly broke down and cried as they recounted their truly rending war experiences, especially their own role in the violence then being unleashed against Vietnamese civilians. They were appalled by the part that they had willingly played just months earlier, and angered by the lies they heard elected Washington leaders telling the American people about how well the war was going since their return home. They had become determined to speak out, partly as patriots of conscience, partly in atonement for what they had done as soldiers. They became activists in the very influential movement of anti–Vietnam War veterans that did a great deal to bring this ugly chapter in U.S. history to an end. It was one of the most moving evenings I have ever spent because of such powerful and authentic testimony, a blending of pain and truthfulness. One of these young men was Kenneth Campbell, author of this book. We have remained in contact ever since, and the inspirational trajectory of his subsequent development has reached a point of culmination, at least for now, in the pages that follow.

It is a matter of vital national and human concern, not idle curiosity, why so few soldiers reacted to Vietnam in a similar manner. After all, Ken Campbell went to Vietnam as a typical U.S. patriot eager to support a war effort that he believed at the time to be a necessary part of the struggle against an expansionist world communist movement being orchestrated by Moscow. He was not then, nor did he ever become, alienated from the American mainstream. In this book he reserves equally harsh comments for the viewpoints he associates with the extremes of left and right. Campbell's anger against the Vietnam War has not abated over the decades, and he is newly disillusioned about the U.S. political process, yet more convinced than ever that what this country needs desperately is elected leaders and appointed officials who believe that the American people are always entitled to know the truth and who do not stumble or rush into wars that are not in every sense of the word *necessary*. For Campbell a necessary war is either fought for the sake of human solidarity to rescue a people being victimized by genocide or essentially undertaken in defense of the country against an aggressive enemy. He vividly contrasts his father's experience in World War II, a war he affirms as a just and exemplary struggle, with his own eventual repudiation of the Vietnam War as not only unjust, but in its essence a criminal enterprise foisted on the American people by deceit, and additionally, inflicting immeasurable suffering on a distant people who posed no dire threat to humanity or to the United States.

In this spirit Campbell affirms the initial response after the September 11 attacks that launched a war against Afghanistan, because he regarded the al-Qaeda threat as sufficiently menacing to warrant a defensive war in response. But when the U.S. government invaded Iraq in 2003, it crossed a bright red line in Campbell's political and moral imagination that recalled the personal ordeal and national tragedy that was the Vietnam War.

A terrifying aspect of this baleful repetition is its depressing revelation that the lessons of Vietnam, once seemingly so vivid as to be labeled by militarists as "the Vietnam syndrome," have been forgotten (or possibly never truly learned), and the mistakes and crimes committed back then are again taking place on a massive scale in another distant non-Western country. As Campbell reminds us, the extreme right never was willing to acknowledge the wrongdoing, or even the failures, of the Vietnam era, lamely explaining U.S. defeat and humiliation as solely a consequence of a stab in the back at home by the liberal media and their friends in high places, especially among the Democratic Party faithful.

The neoconservative cabal that has been in control of the U.S. government since the 2000 presidential elections seized upon the climate of patriotic fervor that existed immediately after 9/11 to pursue its preplanned grand strategy, which had been for years committed above all else to transforming the political landscape of the Middle East by military means, which meant getting rid of any government in the region that was regarded as anti-American or anti-Israeli. The Iraq War fit this regional scenario far better than that of an essential step taken for the sake of counterterrorism. As such, the confrontation with Saddam Hussein's Iraq was tainted with cynical deception from its outset. It produced a *necessary* set of lies told by the highest U.S. government officials to validate an *unnecessary* war, sending young Americans overseas to kill and to die on false pretenses.

Even if the military mission had been just, necessary, and feasible, and no physical or mental injury resulted from participation in combat, the human costs for the soldiers would have been high, reinforcing the elementary message that for selfish reasons alone war should be truly treated as an option of last resort. Campbell's depiction of the sadistic character of the military training he received in the United States before being shipped to Vietnam is chilling. His depiction of a U.S. boot camp at Parris Island, South Carolina, makes it unsurprising, yet still shocking, that while in the combat zone of Vietnam, his nightmares were not about the battlefield risks he was then daily facing, but consistently hearkened back to the cruelties he experienced and witnessed during those weeks of training prior to being sent out to fight.

Campbell relies on the metaphor of "quagmire" to connect these two wars of national disgrace together. In both wars the security rationale was contrived by politicians to convince a rather passive citizenry. The government and their voluntary accomplices in media and think tanks, then as now, relied on cooked evidence, inflammatory allegations, and politicized intelligence assessments. In neither Vietnam nor Iraq was there any provocation or threat by the "enemy" that might explain the U.S. recourse of war in response. Also, U.S. war aims kept shifting as the earlier goals came to be seen as irrelevant or unattainable. In both instances, the political leaders persisted with the engagement in the war long after there was no chance of winning, shamelessly allowing the casualty figures to rise on both sides for no legitimate reason. In a sense, the quagmire was not so much a characteristic of the war zone as it was an expression of *political* self-entrapment. The entrapment resulted from earlier claims whose falsity would be exposed if failure were to be admitted, and the human sacrifices and other costs incurred would be revealed as pointless. To avoid taking responsibility most politicians defer exposing their deceit as long as possible, hopefully shifting the main burden of acknowledgment to a new leadership. Finally, a rising tide of opposition at home and deepening failure abroad give the government little choice but to change course. By then, it is likely to be much too late to make a graceful exit. Humiliation and recriminations inevitably follow, and if the Vietnam pattern repeats itself in Iraq, politicians will do their best to pin the blame on the top military brass. This might be more difficult to do in the Iraq setting, because there has been a chorus of harsh anti-Rumsfeld criticism from within the military, which finally resulted in his resignation.

With admirable clarity, Campbell depicts this tale of two demoralizing military misadventures in such a manner as to give a reader deep insight into why such "wars of choice" are doomed to fail. But he does more than this. He combines in an original way first-rate analysis of what went wrong strategically with a moving account of what it meant to be a soldier caught up in the existential drama of the ordeal. The result is a creative new genre of war commentary: part memoir, part political science, with an important dialogue between these two modes of knowing—reason and experience.

Reflecting on the comparison of the two wars, there is little doubt that both gave rise to a condition of political quagmire that delayed and complicated the process of extrication. There are important differences that need to be noted, as well. In Vietnam, the main adversary was a government, although when the United States was seriously ready to negotiate, it reluctantly allowed the insurgent movement, the National Liberation Front, to take part in the negotiations. In Iraq, it remains difficult to identify who might represent the insurgency. In Vietnam, the war was confined to Vietnam, although there were risks of escalation involving China, but to the extent that the "war against terror" has been insinuated into the Iraq context, there is always the risk that the vulnerability of the United States exposed on 9/11 will lead to a second devastating attack. In Vietnam, the leadership of both political parties in the United States, although somewhat mired in anticommunist ideology, subscribed to a realist foreign policy, which was mindful of Soviet countervailing power and ready to craft a diplomatic stance based on national interests rather than to insist on pursuing an evangelical agenda based on a struggle against evil.

Every American at all levels of society can benefit from this book, but it is especially valuable for young Americans who need to ponder these national traumas so as to make their recurrence in the future less likely. In a fundamental sense, Campbell is making an appeal for an informed and engaged citizenry that demands transparency from its government and insists on holding leaders accountable. He is hopeful about the self-correcting potential of our democracy. *A Tale of Two Quagmires* is an excellent book by an excellent person!

Richard Falk
Santa Monica, California

PREFACE

I wrote this book because I was dissatisfied with the quality of the debate over the analogy of Vietnam and the Iraq War. Although I knew from personal experience that there were some critical similarities between the Vietnam and Iraq Wars, the arguments both against and sometimes for this position tended to be superficial. It seemed to me that those arguing the most passionately against the Vietnam analogy often knew the least about Vietnam.

I served in Vietnam during the worst year of the war (1968–1969), in the most dangerous area of country (the I Corps), in a job that had one of the highest mortality rates in combat (artillery forward observer). Having barely survived that experience and having learned what that war was actually about, I came home with a hunger to learn more about the politics of war and an obligation, as a survivor, to teach others about my experiences. I eventually joined other Vietnam veterans in opposing the Vietnam War and was with John Kerry and the Vietnam Veterans Against the War at the Winter Soldier Investigation in Detroit in January 1971, and at "Operation Dewey Canyon III" on the Capitol Mall in April 1971.

I earned a B.A. in history from Temple University in 1976. For the next several years, I worked as a quality control inspector in factories, as a spray painter in a shipyard, as a bus driver, a taxi driver, and a respiratory therapy technician in a hospital. I eventually returned to Temple to earn an M.A. and a Ph.D. in political science, and for the past twenty years I have taught a course on the lessons of Vietnam, first as an adjunct professor at Villanova, then as an assistant and an associate professor at the University of Delaware. I wrote my dissertation at Temple on the military's lessons of Vietnam and was fortunate to have the dean of America's military historians, the late Russell Weigley, on my dissertation committee. (The only other dissertation on the military's lessons of Vietnam, at that time, was written at Princeton by Major David Petraeus, who went on to become, according to Thomas Ricks's outstanding book, *Fiasco,* an exceptionally wise, ethical, and effective general in the current Iraq War.)[1]

When the United States invaded Iraq in 2003 and the Vietnam analogy was raised, I knew that only those with significant knowledge of the Vietnam War could do the question justice. I decided, therefore, to write this book. I have kept it short and free of academic jargon, because I want students, policy makers, and the general public to know what I know. I begin with a condensed version of my Vietnam combat experience and the very personal lessons I drew from it. Then I examine the nature of a "quagmire"—the military intervention that seems so easy to enter, but so difficult to exit—and the step-by-step process that political and military leaders take the nation through in making and sustaining a quagmire: entering, sinking deeper, hitting bottom, and blocking the exit. I then examine the Vietnam quagmire, explore its many conflicting lessons, and compare it with the Iraq quagmire. Finally, I discuss the problems and prospects of getting out of Iraq and avoiding new quagmires in the future. I have tried, in my research, to use only the highest-quality sources: recognized leading scholars, official government documents (many only recently declassified), widely respected policy analysts, and the words of the policy makers themselves.

I had much assistance in this project. I first must thank the many students I have taught over the past twenty years, and from whom I have learned. I must also thank my mentors at Temple University: Lynn Miller (international law and organization), Peter Bachrach (democratic theory), and Harry Bailey (the presidency). They were truly great teachers. I must also thank my undergraduate research assistants, Kristen Lindell, Laura Yayac, and Zach Schafer. I would also like to thank the anonymous sender of those declassified CIA files on Vietnam that one day recently appeared in my office mailbox in a plain brown envelope without a return address or note. Those files were most helpful.

I also wish to express deep appreciation to Bill Ehrhart for permitting me to reprint his poem, to Richard Falk for writing his wonderful foreword, and to Jennifer Knerr for quickly seeing the value in publishing my book and supporting me so well through the process. Finally, I thank my best editor and toughest critic, my wife, Cathy, for her help, her patience, and her love. Of course, any mistakes herein are entirely my fault.

Kenneth J. Campbell

A Tale of Two Quagmires

ONE

~∞∞∞~

THE GREAT DEBATE

I don't want to talk about Vietnam.
This is not Vietnam. This is Iraq!
—*L. Paul Bremer*

Is Iraq another Vietnam? This question has triggered fierce debate throughout the United States over the past couple of years, and as the Iraq War continues to drag on with no end in sight, the ferocity of the debate has intensified. The national debate over the Vietnam analogy and the Iraq War began with the emergence of the Iraqi insurgency, following the U.S. invasion and occupation of Iraq in 2003. As it became clear that the Iraqi resistance was more than a few "dead-enders" and "Saddamist holdouts," domestic critics of the U.S. war began to raise the specter of another Vietnam. They argued that Iraq was becoming another quagmire from which the United States will eventually have to withdraw, again, in humiliation and defeat.

Supporters of the war rejected the Vietnam comparison and urged proponents of the analogy to "get over" Vietnam. They contended that there were great differences between the two wars and that, unlike in Vietnam, U.S. forces in Iraq would ul-

1

timately prevail. As the Iraq War dragged on through the next three years, the costs in lives and resources rose steadily, as did the volume and intensity of the debate over the Vietnam analogy. Partisans on both sides of the debate believe passionately that they are right, but where is the truth? Are Iraq and Vietnam more similar or more different? And what criteria do we use to judge? The following is a brief examination of some of the best arguments, proffered by some of the best representatives of the two sides of this debate.

NO, IRAQ IS *NOT* VIETNAM!

Professors Jeffrey Record and Andrew Terrill present a very professional and detailed critique of the Vietnam analogy for the U.S. Army War College. Professor Record was a civilian pacification specialist in Vietnam and is now a national security specialist at the U.S. Air War College in Alabama. Professor Terrill was a career military officer and is now a Middle East specialist at the U.S. Army War College in Pennsylvania. These authors bring an unusual combination of academic training and practical experience to their examination of the Vietnam analogy. In their study they reach the following conclusion:

> Careful examination of the evidence reveals that the differences between the two conflicts greatly outnumber the similarities. This is especially true in the strategic and military dimensions of the two wars. There is simply no comparison between the strategic environment, the scale of military operations, the scale of losses incurred, the quality of the enemy resistance, the role of the enemy allies, and the duration of combat.[1]

However, the authors do include an important caveat: "Such an emphatic judgment, however, may not apply to at least two aspects of the political dimensions of the Iraq and Vietnam wars: attempts at state-building in an alien culture, and sustaining domestic political support in a protracted war against an irregular enemy."[2] Record and Terrill also add an important qualification to their case against comparing Iraq to Vietnam: "The question of whether the Iraq War of 2003 was a war of necessity is one of the key factors bearing on the political sustainability of the ongoing U.S. effort to create a stable, prosperous, and democratic Iraq."[3] The authors do not elaborate on the question of the necessity for the Iraq War. Rather, they appear to accept at face value the Bush administration's justification for the Iraq War as "part of the larger war on terrorism that was sparked by the horrendous al-Qaeda attacks on the United States of September 11, 2001."[4]

One of the most influential critiques of the Vietnam analogy, at least among the intellectual community, is Christopher Hitchens's *Slate* magazine article published in early 2005. In this piece, Hitchens writes that Iraq and Vietnam have "nothing whatsoever in common."[5] He contends that, unlike Ho Chi Minh, who emulated the words of Thomas Jefferson and had been an ally of the West, Iraqi insurgents descended from those who took the side of the Axis powers during World War II and now oppose democratic elections on principle. Hitchens goes on to assert that Ho Chi Minh's Vietnam never invaded its neighbor, never committed genocide, and never sought weapons of mass destruction, as Saddam Hussein's Iraq had. Hitchens insists that in Vietnam, the Americans committed the worst atrocities, while in Iraq, Saddam and his followers committed the worst atrocities. He points out that in Vietnam during the Kennedy years, the United States favored the Roman Catholic minority, whereas in Iraq, the United States now takes a more ecumenical approach to religious differences. Finally, Christopher Hitchens labels those who see an analogy between Iraq and Vietnam as "narrow," "shallow," and "third rate."[6]

Next we have Melvin Laird's late 2005 piece in *Foreign Affairs.* Laird was President Nixon's secretary of defense from 1969 to 1973. In his article, Laird states: "The War in Iraq is not 'another Vietnam,'" but could become one if we fail to learn the lessons of Vietnam. For Laird, the chief lesson of Vietnam is that the policy of "Vietnamization" succeeded and that a similar policy of "Iraqization" can work just as well in Iraq. He goes on to contend that "the truth about Vietnam that revisionist historians conveniently forget is that the United States had not lost when we withdrew in 1973. In fact, we grabbed defeat from the jaws of victory two years later when Congress cut off the funding for South Vietnam that had allowed it to continue to fight on its own." Furthermore, Laird argues: "The shame of Vietnam is not that we were there in the first place, but that we betrayed our ally in the end. It was Congress that turned its back on the promises of the Paris accord."[7]

However, at another point in the article, Laird describes America's Saigon ally as "corrupt, selfish men who were no more than dictators in the garb of statesmen." He then proceeds to list the many ways that Iraq *is* like Vietnam:

- "Both the Vietnam War and the Iraq war were launched based on intelligence failures and possible outright deception."
- Both began as self-defense and "morphed into nation-building."
- In both wars, "Our presence is what feeds the insurgency."
- In Vietnam, "Countless innocent civilians were killed in the indiscriminate hunt for Vietcong among the South Vietnamese peasantry. Our volunteer troops in Iraq are better trained and supervised, yet the potential remains for the slaughter of the innocents."
- "As with Vietnam, the Iraq war is revealing chinks in our fiscal armor. Only after the Vietnam War ended did its drain on the U.S. economy become apparent."
- In both wars, most of our closest Western allies refused to join the fight.
- "Americans will not be lied to ... as with the Vietnam War, if necessary they will take to the streets to be heard."

- "Just as the spread of communism was very real in the 1960s, so the spread of radical fundamentalist Islam is very real today."[8]

Laird lobbies for continuing the war of "nation-building" in Iraq in part by citing the alleged connection between the Iraq War and 9/11: "Bush has the opportunity to reshape the region. 'Nation-building' is not an epithet or a slogan. After the attacks of September 11, 2001, it is our duty."[9]

Finally, defense policy specialist Stephen Biddle rejects the Vietnam analogy in an article in the March/April 2006 issue of *Foreign Affairs* called "Seeing Baghdad, Thinking Saigon."[10] Biddle determines the primary nature of the Iraq War to be a civil war and its secondary nature to be an insurgency against a foreign (U.S.) occupation. Therefore, Biddle contends, the strategy of "Iraqization"—modeled on "Vietnamization" thirty years ago—is the wrong strategy to adopt, because in a civil war, turning over the responsibility for security to indigenous military and police forces will only make the civil war worse. Instead, Biddle contends that U.S. troops must remain in the middle of the civil war in Iraq and attempt to "cap" the communal violence until Iraq's many political and religious factions can work out an accommodation at some point in the future.

YES, IRAQ *IS* VIETNAM!

Daniel Ellsberg, a former Marine officer, civilian Vietnam adviser, and purloiner of the top-secret *Pentagon Papers,* said in remarks made at a Capitol Hill briefing in 2005 that Iraq was similar to Vietnam for several reasons. First, the United States had no real chance of winning in either war because in both cases, the indigenous population viewed the United States as an illegitimate foreign occupier. Second, both wars were sustained by a lie and a charge. The "lie" was that the United States was in both wars to spread "democracy," when the real reason was imperial dominance. The "charge" was that in both wars, calling for immediate withdrawal was an act of "cowardice," when in fact it was an act of courage. Because of these lies and charges, the Vietnam War dragged on far longer with higher costs than it might otherwise have. This, Ellsberg contends, is also true of the Iraq War.[11]

To Sir Lawrence Freedman, professor of war studies at King's College in London and an internationally respected expert on military strategy, Iraq is similar to Vietnam in that both wars took on the public face of the secretaries of defense running them. To Lawrence Freedman, Robert McNamara and Donald Rumsfeld share the characteristic of personal arrogance in their refusal to heed the advice of their generals. And Freedman believes that, as in Vietnam, launching a war without direct provocation and bogging the United States down in a bungled war in Iraq will leave the United States weaker, not stronger, meaning that Rumsfeld will have left behind an "Iraq syndrome" just as McNamara left behind a "Vietnam syndrome."[12]

U.S. Senator Chuck Hagel, a Republican from Nebraska and a former squad leader in Vietnam, said that a "parallel" was emerging between Vietnam and Iraq. He said: "The longer we stay in Iraq, the more similarities will start to develop, meaning essentially that we are getting more and more bogged down, taking more and more casualties, more and more heated dissension and debate in the United States."[13]

John Mueller, professor of political science at Ohio State University and author of the 1973 classic study of public opinion and casualties during the Vietnam War, *War, Presidents, and Public Opinion*,[14] wrote in *Foreign Affairs* that just as during Vietnam, as U.S. casualties in Iraq rose, public support fell. And Mueller, too, predicted a lasting "Iraq syndrome," just as there was a lasting "Vietnam syndrome."[15]

Martin van Creveld, an internationally renowned military historian and a professor at Hebrew University, insisted that there are many important parallels between Iraq and Vietnam. He wrote, "The question is no longer if American forces will be withdrawn, but how soon—and at what cost." And Creveld recommended that President Bush and his advisers be put on trial for "misleading the American people" into "the most foolish war since Emperor Augustus in 9 B.C. sent his legions into Germany and lost them."[16]

Finally, Lt. General William Odom (ret.), director of the National Security Agency during the Reagan administration, wrote that of the many similarities between the wars in Iraq and Vietnam, the most important were the use of "phony intelligence" and "confused war aims." He argued, however, that the debacle in Iraq is likely to have far more damaging consequences than did Vietnam to U.S. power in the world.[17]

THE STRATEGIC ESSENCE OF A QUAGMIRE

My own view, having served in the Vietnam War for thirteen months and having studied it for thirty years, is that on the most important level—the strategic political level—Iraq and Vietnam are *exactly* alike. Both wars were constructed upon, and sustained by, a quicksand of conscious political deception. As such, they were and are *quagmires.* No matter how many differences there are between Vietnam and Iraq—and there are many—the fact that their strategic political character is identical means that the Iraq War will end in failure, just as Vietnam did more than thirty years ago. So it is not a question of *whether* the United States will lose the war in Iraq; the war was lost the day the Bush administration decided to invade Iraq. The question is, how much more are Americans prepared to pay for a lost war? In Vietnam, the "tipping point" when the majority of Americans realized the war in Vietnam was not worth fighting came in early 1968, after the Tet Offensive, but it took U.S. leaders five more years to withdraw U.S. troops from Vietnam. The cost for this delay was 20,000 more American lives, 300,000 more Vietnamese lives, and many billions of U.S. tax dollars. It would be unwise to repeat this mistake in Iraq and to delay withdrawal.

According to the *American Heritage Dictionary,* a *quagmire* is "a bog having a surface that yields when stepped on," or "a difficult or precarious situation from which extrication is almost impossible."[18] The first is a physical quagmire; the second is a politico-military quagmire. No one in his or her right mind would intentionally enter a physical quagmire, as it could mean his or her death. If an individual enters a physical quagmire, it is because he or she is deceived by God or Mother Nature into believing that the quagmire's *surface* is solid enough to support a person's weight. However, once entered, it soon becomes apparent to the person that the surface of the quagmire is quite soft, and he or she begins sinking deeper and deeper into mortal danger.

This is also true for a politico-military quagmire. No rational nation enters a quagmire intentionally. If a nation sends its troops into a quagmire, it is because its leaders have deceived the people and the troops of the nation into believing that the war is necessary. However, once in the quagmire, it gradually begins to dawn on the people and the troops that the original *purpose* for the war is highly suspect and the nation is sinking deeper and deeper into mortal danger.

Lawrence Freedman has traced the quagmire metaphor back to the Western Front during World War I, where soldiers on both sides were bogged down in the mud and the trenches of a protracted, wasteful war. Then, in the late 1940s and early 1950s, according to Professor Freedman, the quagmire metaphor was applied to the French in Vietnam, where they had become bogged down in their attempt to reimpose colonial rule by military force. The first U.S. use of the metaphor was by journalist David Halberstam in his 1964 book, *The Making of a Quagmire*. In his book, Halberstam examined the already floundering U.S. military intervention in Vietnam.[19] But how are quagmires "made"? How does one enter a quagmire? Better yet, how does one exit a quagmire?

THE QUAGMIRE PROCESS

All wars are attempts to resolve political disputes between nations and peoples by brute force. In this sense, war is uncivilized, bestial behavior. It is also quite often self-destructive. Thus, except in rare circumstances, war is foolish behavior. These are the lessons the world learned the hard way in World War I.[20] The rare circumstances when war is necessary and prudent are when a nation must defend itself against an unprovoked attack—such as Pearl Harbor—and when a helpless population must be rescued from genocidal extermination—such as the Holocaust. These are the lessons the world learned the hard way from World War II.[21] Therefore, the international community has for a hundred years legally prohibited and morally condemned *unnecessary* war.[22] "What does all this have to do with a quagmire?" you might ask. Well, it's really quite simple. If it is taboo in today's world to wage an unnecessary war, then leaders who nevertheless intend to wage an unnecessary war must first fool their nation's people and troops into believing the war is really necessary. They must employ massive *deception.*

Quagmires are built upon the quicksand of deception, deception about *purpose, progress, methods,* and *exit.* When the nation's leaders conceive of a war for a questionable *purpose,* they deceptively portray it as a "just cause," because they know that the people of the nation will not long support an unnecessary war and that the nation's troops will not long risk their lives for an unnecessary war. Once the nation's leaders have tricked the people and the troops into a quagmire, the leaders then employ more deception to convince the people and the troops that the leaders' strategy is actually producing the predicted *progress.* These leaders then use further deception to cover up their illegal and immoral *methods* for fighting the war, such as torturing detainees and killing innocent civilians. Finally, when the people and the troops begin to suspect that the war is a mistake—as they will inevitably do—the nation's leaders block the quagmire's *exit* by using deception to convince the people and the troops that withdrawal is not a realistic option.

However, once the people and the troops discover their leaders' massive deception—as again, they will inevitably do—the people's trust in their leaders will evaporate quickly, and the morale of the troops will fall dangerously. The only solution to such a national nightmare is *quagmire extraction.* This process requires national democratic action by the public, interest groups, the media, Congress, political parties, and the troops themselves. This democratic action must expose the massive deception and emphasize the inevitable waste of more lives, tax dollars, and national reputation, if the troops are not withdrawn and the war ended quickly.

In analyzing this very difficult and controversial problem, I have combined my personal experience as a young man in combat in Vietnam with my scholarly knowledge gained over three decades of academic research, teaching and publishing on the politics of war. I have drawn supportive evidence for my arguments from what I believe are the most credible sources from academia, government, think tanks, and the media. Although perfect objectivity is humanly impossible, especially regarding highly controversial issues such as the one discussed in this book, I have tried my best to be fair. What the reader will encounter herein certainly is not perfect wisdom, but it is the best I can provide at this time. I hope it helps.

TWO

Personal Encounter with a Quagmire

Ask not what your country can do for you.
Ask what you can do for your country.
—John F. Kennedy

PHILLY CORNER BOY

I was born in Temple University Hospital in North Philadelphia on July 3, 1949. I grew up in a working-class neighborhood of North Philadelphia called Hunting Park. My father was a book-keeper for a small firm that manufactured lawn and golf supplies. My mother was a typical 1950s housewife. Dad earned his bachelor's degree from Temple University via the GI Bill after he "flew a desk" (Mom's description) for the U.S. Eighth Air Force during World War II. He was an office clerk for the 36th Bombardment Squadron, which specialized in radar countermeasures and was stationed at Alconbury, England. Dad was proud of his service and would often show me his old Army Air Corps uniform, hanging in the mothballed garment bag in the basement.

Dad in England (1944)

My father's parents were born to Irish Catholic farmers from Tyrone and Donegal, and they "came over on the boat" during the first decade of the twentieth century. Mom's father was from a Scots-Irish Protestant family of coal mining engineers from the Wilkes-Barre area of Pennsylvania, and her mother was a "Pennsylvania Dutch" Protestant from the Susquehanna River valley north of Harrisburg. Mom and Dad met at a dance in Philadelphia, and she converted to Catholicism to marry him.

Despite my father's college degree, we were one of the poorest families on our street of mostly cops, firemen, bus drivers, construction workers, and factory workers. We never owned a car or went on a summer vacation. My parents had five kids to feed, and my dad's tendency to drink part of his paycheck on the way home from work made paying the bills difficult for Mom.

I was the second born, with brother Gerry two years older. A sister, Joan—"the rose between the thorns," as Mom loved to call her—and two more brothers, Lary and Mike, eventually followed me. I went to St. Henry's parochial school, became an altar boy, a Cub Scout, a newspaper carrier, and a Little League baseball player. I also got into fistfights, as I was skinny, pigeon-

Little gunslinger (1954)

Altar boy (1963)

toed, and wore glasses from the age of seven. I hated fighting and lost most, but never backed down from one.

I began smoking cigarettes at the age of ten, working part time at eleven, and drinking whiskey at twelve. I hung on the street corners singing "doo-wop," broke into the occasional box-car, but managed to stay out of any real trouble. In high school, I was a *C* student with *A* potential. I had been expected to follow my Benedictine uncle into the priesthood, but I started going to dances on the weekends—Boulevard on Friday nights, Wagner's on Sunday afternoons—and started dating girls, so those plans were derailed.

My father was passionately political and as right wing as the day is long. If he wasn't a member of the John Birch Society, he was cheating them out of dues. My father's heroes were Senator Joe McCarthy, General Douglas MacArthur, FBI Director J. Edgar Hoover, and the right-wing radio priest Father Coughlin. I remember Dad being glued to the little black and white television in the early fifties, watching the Army McCarthy Hearings. Dad was convinced that the government was riddled with communists. He also loved to listen to MacArthur's "Farewell Address" over and over again on the record player. When I was fourteen, my father gave me a copy of *None Dare Call It Treason*, which enlightened me on the evils of the "world communist conspiracy." Although Dad advised me never to argue about politics or religion in a bar when I grew up, he was frequently thrown out of bars for doing just that.

In 1965, my father was diagnosed with cancer and given six months to live. He lingered eleven months and died on July 5, 1966, weighing just fifty-six pounds. On July 5, 1967, three weeks after graduating from Cardinal Dougherty High School and exactly one year after my father's death, I left for Parris Island, South Carolina. I joined the Marines because I wanted to go to Vietnam and come back a hero, and because I had seen every John Wayne movie. I also figured the Marines would make me "tough," make me a "man." I also wanted desperately to get out of the neighborhood, see the world, and do something exciting with my life.

VOLUNTEER FOR AMERICA

"See Parris and die." I hated boot camp! The Marine drill instructors seemed cruel and sadistic, often engaging in malicious physical and mental abuse, and enjoying it. They created a hell at Parris Island and used fear to intimidate recruits: fear of physical beatings (which were frequent), fear of social isolation, and fear of never getting off the island. During the ten weeks I was there, our senior drill instructor punched each of the eighty-six recruits in my platoon in the stomach while we stood at attention because of mistakes we made on the drill field. Our rifle range instructor knocked a recruit from my platoon unconscious, causing him to go into convulsions. And a recruit from the platoon ahead of ours on the pistol range put his .45 under his chin and blew the top of his head off.

I will admit that Marine boot camp taught me some valuable lifelong lessons about discipline, tenacity, and physical fitness. Nevertheless, Parris Island so traumatized me that my post-Vietnam nightmares were never about being back in Vietnam; they were about being back on Parris Island.

I did manage to get through basic training without my drill instructors learning my name. Anonymity was a good thing. Any personal attention from those drill instructors usually meant bad attention. At the end of basic, upon graduation, we newly minted Marines were given our MOSes, or military occupational specialties. Riflemen, or "grunts," were designated 0311. I was designated 0846, which meant that I was to be trained as a forward artillery scout observer—an "arty FO"—responsible for calling in artillery fire in support of a rifle company. When the senior drill instructor read out my name and MOS, he informed me that an artillery FO had the third-highest mortality rate in the Marine Corps, exceeded only by radiomen and machine-gunners. It seems the enemy liked to knock out a company's communications, automatic weapons, and support fire early. I was not encouraged.

After twenty days' leave, I was sent to FO school at Camp Pendleton, California. Thirty of us attended a four-week course during which we learned how to read maps, use a compass, communicate on a radio, and adjust artillery fire on old, rusted car bodies. Much to my surprise, I was good at it. I graduated first in my class. During these four weeks, I became close friends with two Marines, Wayne Bernhardt from Queens and Gary "Ugly Hog" Smith from Kentucky. Gary's girlfriend always addressed his letters to "PFC Gary Ugly Hog Smith" to tease him about his rather large size. Once, as a joke, she sent him a pair of boxer shorts so big that both of us could fit in them.

Home from boot camp

Upon graduation from FO school in December 1967, our class was split up and one half sent to Camp Lejeune, North Carolina, to await orders to Vietnam. The other half stayed at Camp Pendleton awaiting orders. Wayne, Gary, and I were sent to Lejeune. Three weeks later, Wayne received his orders. I then volunteered for orders to Vietnam so that we could go over together. Gary received his orders a bit later and soon followed us to Vietnam. Wayne and I visited each other while on leave before going to Vietnam. During those twenty days, Wayne dated my sister. (Both Wayne Bernhardt and Gary Smith were killed in action in Vietnam, Wayne by a booby trap and Gary by a sniper.)

While Wayne and I were on leave, the Tet Offensive began, and I watched the early days of the fierce fighting on television at home. This was not good. On February 4, 1968, Wayne and I reported to Staging Battalion at Camp Pendleton, California. This was preparation for going to Vietnam and involved four weeks of specialized training. Our staging company consisted of a mix of rookies and "old salts" going back for their second or third tour. The latter made up about 10 percent of the company. We rookies listened closely to the combat veterans, as though they were offering "burning bush" wisdom. The common advice they gave us was to "throw the book away" when we got to Vietnam, because the official rules would likely get us killed. Be tough and ruthless or come home in a body bag.

We received classes in Vietnamese culture, the spreading "Red Menace" of Asian communism, booby traps, ambushes, escape and evasion, and the Geneva Conventions. One class consisted of a U.S. government documentary called *Why Vietnam?* Throughout the film, LBJ's voice kept asking, "Why Vietnam?" The narrator explained that we were fighting in South Vietnam because the vast majority of the Vietnamese people wanted us there to save them from the evil communists. I remember a sergeant instructor teaching us how to set up an L-shaped ambush. After ensuring that all officers were out of earshot, the sergeant urged us to use shotguns at close range in an ambush and to bring along machetes or hatchets to chop up the bodies of the enemy we killed. He assured us from his experience in Vietnam that this was an effective method of instilling terror into the hearts of the enemy who found the remains of their buddies. (Many years later, as I was reading Phil Caputo's war classic, *A Rumor of War,* I couldn't help but wonder if we had the same ambush class instructor. He describes a Marine sergeant entering the classroom, burying a hatchet in the wooden wall, and leading the class in a chant: "Ambushes are murder and murder is fun!")[1]

The escape-and-evasion class was particularly gruesome. The sergeant instructor began by explaining in a soothing voice the importance of staying alive in the jungle, all the while petting a white rabbit he was cradling in his lap. Suddenly, he broke the rabbit's neck, took out a knife, skinned the rabbit, gutted it, and threw its internal organs into the audience, hitting some Marines in the face. He explained that this shocking demonstration was intended to "harden" us to the gore of combat.[2]

The Geneva Conventions class consisted largely of issuing us our Geneva Convention wallet cards and instructing us on how to behave in the event we were captured. The sergeant in charge of this class also advised us to cut the corners off the card so that if we were captured, we could "shove them up our asses," because, according to this instructor, that's all they would be good for. I recall little or nothing said about how to treat enemy prisoners. The class on booby traps used models of punji-stake pits, spiked swinging gates, and other crude devices common in the early years of the war. (Unfortunately, as we soon learned, these crude devices were obsolete by 1968, as by then the Viet Cong possessed so much U.S. ordnance that they routinely constructed their booby traps with U.S. hand grenades, mortar shells, artillery shells, and 250-pound bombs. Use of the latter often made it difficult to determine which appendages belonged to which Marine's body.) On our last weekend of liberty before leaving for Vietnam, Wayne and I went up to Los Angeles and caught the recently released movie *Bonnie and Clyde*. I remember on the way into the theater, we tried to impress the pretty young cashier by describing ourselves as "underage, oversexed, teenage killers." It didn't work.

TO THE 'NAM

After a three-day stopover in Okinawa, we landed in Da Nang on February 29. From there, Wayne and I were split up and sent to different units in separate parts of the I Corps. Although by early 1968, South Vietnam was virtually overrun with U.S. troops, U.S. bases, U.S. weapons, U.S. technology, and so on, the "tail-to-tooth" ratio was approximately 6:1, which meant that only 15 percent of all U.S. troops in Vietnam were engaged in sustained ground combat operations. The remaining 85 percent were "in support" as truck drivers, supply clerks, airplane mechanics, military police, medical technicians, and so on. Wayne and I were headed to join the 15 percent in combat: the "tip of the spear," Marine grunt companies. I was sent first to "A" Battery, 1st Battalion, 11th Marine Regiment, 1st Marine Division (Alpha 1/11) at Phu Bai. I was then assigned to scout for "B" Company, 1st Battalion, 1st Marine Regiment, 1st Marine Division (Bravo 1/1). Bravo Company was at that time mopping up after their monthlong battle to retake Hue. While I waited in Phu Bai for Bravo Company to return, I had my Zippo lighter inscribed with what I considered a deep thought: "To really live, you must nearly die." Yep, I was a philosopher.

UP NORTH

The first half of my thirteen-month tour in Vietnam was spent along the DMZ, humping up and down the jungle-covered mountains around Khe Sanh and patrolling the defoliant-denuded plateau around Con Thien. We were sent "up north" after the Tet Offensive to relieve the siege of Khe Sanh, which had been surrounded and pounded by the NVA (North Vietnamese Army) for more than two months. I was happy that I had missed the worst fighting of the Tet Offensive, especially in Hue, but now we seemed to be going from the proverbial frying pan into the fire. The NVA were tough, well-trained, heavily armed, uniformed soldiers who often engaged us in pitched battles for fixed positions constructed with World War I–like trenches and bunkers. Civilians in the mountainous areas were rare and usually not Vietnamese, but darker-skinned, more primitive, hill tribe minorities. The French called them *montagnards* or "mountain people." We also had to deal with leeches, mosquitoes, rats, poisonous snakes, poisonous centipedes, rock apes, tigers, tropical heat, monsoon rains, and typhoons. We were poorly resupplied in the mountains and often went hungry and thirsty. The priorities were ammunition first, water second, and food third. (Clean clothes, mail, and other such amenities were not priorities.) You could live weeks without food, days without water, but only seconds without ammunition.

It was common to fill our canteens in streams and rivers, if we were lucky enough to come across them. When desperate, we would stake out our dusty ponchos, with the hoods tied shut, to collect rain from a sudden afternoon shower. Then we would carefully drain the water into our canteens, dirt and all. In essence, our digestive systems "went native." We threw away our water purification tablets, and we would tell FNGs ("fucking new guys") who asked how many purification tablets to use: "One if it's clear, two if it's muddy, three if it's bloody." We used dark humor to cope.

We went without washing or shaving for weeks at a time because of chronic water shortages. We never had any spare jungle utilities (the Army called them "fatigues"), so we had to wear the same filthy rags for months at a time. No one in the field ever wore underpants, as they would quickly get funky and cause health problems in unmentionable areas. (This may be the origin of the contemporary phrase "going commando.") We routinely suffered from heatstroke, dysentery, malaria, trench foot, and jungle rot. We became like mountain goats, humping up and down the mountains near the Laotian border. We "shit-canned" (trashed) anything we did not absolutely need to carry. We lost body weight and shed dead weight. We were a half step removed from animals and exhausted all of the time. But when we made "contact" with the enemy, the adrenaline kicked in and we fought fiercely for our lives.

Bravo Company engaged in several major battles while we were up north. My first was one of the worst. On or about Memorial Day, 1968, in the early morning hours, we ran into a well-dug-in NVA unit a few miles southeast of Khe Sanh. During two hours of fierce fighting, we lost more than half our company: a dozen Marines dead and forty wounded. I had a close call when I started crawling forward through the ten-foot-tall elephant grass

Adjusting artillery fire from Hill 689 (July 1968)

to help out with the wounded. Suddenly, an AK-47 round, fired from only a few yards to my front right, cracked past my ear. My lieutenant then pointed out that we no longer had a right flank and instructed me to get my ass back down the hill to where he was. I complied with enthusiasm.

Another bloody battle took place only a few weeks later on Hill 689, west of Khe Sanh. Our company was lifted by chopper from Hill 881 south onto Hill 689 to assist Delta Company. Delta had been overrun several times and was down to fewer than forty Marines. The rest of the battalion—Alpha, Charlie, and Headquarters Companies—joined us on Hill 689. During our first night on the hill, we were hit by a major NVA attack and our battalion perimeter was breached in several places, resulting in hand-to-hand combat. We had to retake some of our own bunkers and trenches from the NVA to restore the integrity of our perimeter. After several days and nights of on-and-off fighting, and the loss of a couple hundred Marines, we evacuated Hill 689 and gave the entire Khe Sanh area back to the NVA.

We next went to Con Thien, where Bravo Company soon fought another major battle just north of the Marine outpost. It began late one morning in August when the 1st Platoon, out on patrol in an area that had been quiet for weeks, ran into a small ambush and took light casualties. Our company commander then decided that, the next day, the entire company would "sneak up" on the same area from the opposite direction. The next morning, when we approached the area, we began taking mortar and machine-gun fire from our front. Then it also started coming from our left, and soon it was coming from our right as well. A superior enemy force was surrounding us. As if this wasn't bad enough, we started getting pounded by long-range NVA artillery from north of the DMZ. Our casualties were mounting, and we realized that we had to get out of there fast. So the company commander had the forward air controller call in fixed-wing aircraft to lay down a large smoke screen. This obscured the vision of the NVA's artillery scouts and allowed us to grab our dead and wounded and hightail it back to Con Thien.

When the regimental commander learned about this, he was not a happy camper. One of his Marine companies got its butt kicked and run all the way back to Con Thien. Consequently, he decided to drop an entire Marine regiment north of this "hot" area to approach it from the rear. He also decided to send Bravo Company out there again as "bait." But before that, he decided that Bravo Company's artillery scout (me!) needed to go back out there, with only one squad as protection (*sic*) to prep the area with artillery fire. When my company commander informed me of this rather unwelcome news, he seemed to realize that I might not make it back. So, he allowed me to handpick the squad, and I chose the one I thought was the best. I also received permission to leave my radioman, Kermit Fox, behind. I could carry the radio, and I saw no sense in both of us getting killed. Before I left, I borrowed a pair of binoculars. I had plans of my own.

Being a big fan of personal survival, I decided that our little ten-man team didn't need to go the entire way to the "hot" area. (The guys in the squad were already mad at me because, as I later learned, they mistakenly assumed that this "suicide mission" was my idea.) So, when we were just out of sight of Con Thien, but still within the realm of its relative safety, I sat us all down and began calling in my fire mission. I knew well the map coordinates of where we had been the day before, and I could see the general area with the borrowed binoculars. I requested that four batteries of artillery be put at my disposal: two 105 mm batteries, a 155 mm battery, and a 4.2-inch mortar battery. (This was to be the largest, most complex fire mission I ever directed while in Vietnam.) I first determined that the wind was blowing from west to east, so I had the "four deuce" mortar battery fire tear gas on the western edge of the target area. I also had the two 105 batteries fire a textbook "zone and shift" pattern (I actually paid attention in FO school) over the entire area using white phosphorus rounds, and high explosive rounds with variable-time, point-detonating, and delayed fuses. Finally, I had the 155 battery fire our brand new "firecracker" rounds that opened up in downward flight and released many little antipersonnel bombs.

While I was adjusting the artillery, the guys in the squad sat around eating C-rations, reading paperback books, or taking naps. After a while, we began to hear a lot of AK-47 fire. We wondered at whom the NVA could be firing, since there were no U.S. troops anywhere near them. We concluded that, in their panic and confusion, the NVA soldiers must have been firing wildly and perhaps at each other. When the fire mission was completed, we strolled back to the base and reported a job well done.

The next morning, Bravo Company—the "bait"—rode to the "hot" area atop twenty-five tanks, while a Marine regiment—our "rescuers"—landed by helicopter farther north of this area. We circled the tanks, hopped off, dug holes, and fought a nasty all-day battle with the NVA. The Marine regiment that was supposed to come to our rescue got bogged down in battle and never reached us. Near dusk, having lost three tanks and a couple dozen Marines, we climbed back aboard the tanks and returned to Con Thien.

While Bravo Company was in the Con Thien area, we had an encounter with a tiger. On the first night of a platoon-size

Between "incoming" north of Con Thien (August 1968)

sweep, I was taking my customary two-hour turn on radio watch when I received a call from a squad leader in a foxhole on our perimeter. He asked me to wake up the dog handler and tell him that his scout dog was wandering in and out between the foxholes. The sergeant was afraid one of our guys might mistake the dog for an NVA soldier and accidentally shoot it.

Because it was pitch dark, I carefully crawled the short distance to where I thought the dog handler was sleeping. I heard an angry growl even before I could whisper his name. (One never shook another heavily armed, lightly sleeping Marine to wake him. Folks can get shot that way.) The dog handler then asked me what I wanted, and I explained that the guys on the line were complaining that his dog was wandering around our perimeter. The dog handler insisted that was impossible, and in the dark he raised his arm to my face to show me that the dog leash was wrapped around it. He explained that the dog could not possibly have wandered away without dragging him along and that he was quite certain he had not gone on any unscheduled trips.

Convinced by the handler's explanation—and his growling dog—I went back to the radio and informed the squad leader that whatever he and his men had seen, it was not our scout dog. The rest of the night passed uneventfully, but early the next morning, shortly after dawn, we found tiger tracks all around one side of our perimeter. Later that morning, while on patrol, we discovered an old, exposed, empty tiger pit that the NVA had probably dug to trap the same tiger. It seems that tigers are equal-opportunity consumers of humans.

DOWN SOUTH

At the end of August, our battalion was transferred "down south" to the Hoi An area, about ten miles south of Da Nang. Here we had a rear area base camp with a mess hall, hot showers, and a "club" in which we could drink cold beer and listen to music. Compared with up north, this was heaven. My radioman and I moved into the "Comm Shack" (communications shack) with the company's battalion radio operator (Greg Paules), the company radio operator (Jimmy King), and two platoon radio operators (George Chittick and Ken Dunbar).

The Vietnamese civilians living close to our base camp were outwardly friendly and economically dependent on us. However, the farther we ventured into the countryside, the more hostile the population became.

Our enemy in this densely populated, lowland area was the VC (Viet Cong). The VC dressed like civilians and used ambushes, snipers, and booby traps against us. VC guerrillas were divided into two groups. The first group consisted of irregular, part-time VC, farmers by day and fighters by night. They used old, inferior weapons and had few combat skills ... except for making booby traps. At booby trap construction, they were world-class artists! (According to the Defense Department, booby traps accounted for approximately 40 percent of all U.S. casualties during the Vietnam War.) The second group, the hardcore VC, was made up of professional guerrillas who were well-armed, well-disciplined, highly motivated, and expert fighters. Underestimating the hardcore VC often proved fatal. On the other hand, our Vietnamese allies, the ARVN (Army of the Republic of Vietnam) seemed lazy, venal, and distinctly unenthusiastic about fighting the VC. We suspected that the VC had infiltrated many ARVN units. Consequently, we never trusted our ARVN "ally." The following account might help illustrate our problem.

Late one night in the fall of 1968, a hardcore VC unit "hit" Bravo Company's joint, thirty-man Marine/ARVN position just a few miles from our base camp. The position was constructed, against strong ARVN objections, on and around a small Vietnamese cemetery and pagoda, because it was the only dry ground in the area. (We were rather ignorant of and insensitive to Vietnamese culture.)

The attack began when the VC started tossing pebbles at our machine gunner from somewhere in front of his position. When he became sufficiently annoyed, he began conducting "recon by fire" with his machine gun, which immediately gave his position away. A VC guerrilla in another location then decapitated the machine gunner with an RPG (rocket-propelled grenade). Next, the VC took out our command post with their first mortar round, killing both a staff sergeant and a squad leader. By the end of the brief but fierce battle, every Marine in the position had been killed or wounded. Oddly, the ARVN troops suffered not a single casualty. After the first shots were fired, all the ARVN soldiers piled into one ARVN bunker and remained there for the duration of the battle, leaving all the fighting to the Marines. Strangely (or perhaps not so strangely), at the end of the firefight, the overpopulated ARVN bunker was the only one untouched by VC fire. The next morning, when I went out to help reinforce the position, one of the survivors told me that at the height of the battle, he had to restrain another Marine from throwing a grenade into the ARVN bunker.

Our military strategy was based on "body count"; the more, the merrier. Our superiors were happy when we reported a high enemy body count and unhappy when we reported a low or no body count. In our battalion COC (Combat Operations Center) the colonel posted a "Tote Board"—a listing of the week's and month's total body count for each company. The colonel rewarded the company with the highest body count with cases of beer and soda. Individuals with the highest body count for the month would get three days' in-country R&R (rest and relaxation) at China Beach in Da Nang. We also left the "Card of Death" on the bodies of VC that we killed. This was supposed to strike the fear of god in the hearts of the enemy.

Often, we padded our body count with inflated "guess-timates," since we rarely went wandering around in the hedges and tree lines after a firefight looking for dead bodies to count, for fear of tripping booby traps. One day in October, while digging for buried weapons, we found three buried bodies and simply added them to the day's body count.

Bravo Company's "Card of Death"

Booby traps were devastating to our morale. Their trip wires were very difficult to detect in daylight and impossible to see at night. When our unit tripped one, we suffered multiple casualties, but because a booby trap could have been set weeks earlier and the culprit long gone, we had no enemy to shoot back at. At least, up north, we felt as though we had a chance to fight back against our NVA attackers.

In our normal area of operations down south, known as "Dodge City," we took sporadic casualties from booby traps. But when we were temporarily transferred farther south to an area near An Hoa known as "the Arizona Territory," we began tripping booby traps, large and small, every day. The situation became so desperate that the company commander "volunteered" a local farmer at gunpoint to "walk point" for us. The company commander figured either the old man would spot booby traps or would be the first to trip it. This worked well for

Kidnapped farmer, ten minutes before he walked us into an ambush (January 1969)

two days. On the third day, the old farmer walked us right into an ambush.

When the VC initiated the ambush, from our rear and our right flank, they caught our company stretched out single file and exposed in a rice paddy. The front of our column was already in a tree line on one side of the paddy, and the rear was still in a tree line on the opposite side of the paddy. Our column instinctively split in two and made for the cover of the opposite tree lines. During the course of the ensuing firefight, we took several casualties from enemy fire (including two dead), but we suffered many more casualties from three episodes of "friendly fire." The first was from a couple of artillery "short rounds" (the battery faulted "wet powder" from the monsoon rains). The second was from a jet bomber we called in, ironically, as an alternative to the faulty artillery. The pilot dropped his entire load of 250-pound bombs too close to us (he "misunderstood" our instructions). The third was from a medevac chopper we called to take out our casualties from the ambush and the first two incidents of "friendly fire." A door gunner "mistook" our guys in the far tree line for the enemy. I concluded that day that there really is no such thing as "friendly fire"; *if it's coming at you, it's not friendly no matter who fired it!*

When it was all over, we continued in the direction we were headed before the ambush. Late in the afternoon, just before we reached a small village, our "volunteer" point man had us give a wide berth to an area the old man said was heavily booby-trapped. We then went through the village (whose inhabitants gave us hostile glares) and up the slope of a small hill behind it. At that point, the farmer was released, unharmed. We were all "dog tired" from the day's activities and were about to set up on the hill for the night and get some sleep when the company commander received orders from Battalion to return after dark to the area where we had been ambushed early in the day. We were to attempt to turn the tables on the ambushers. So a thoroughly exhausted Bravo Company (or what was left of it) "saddled up," went back down the hill, and back through the village. When we were almost to the area the old farmer said was full of booby traps, the company commander sat us down and waited for darkness. This caused much grumbling up and down the line about the "wisdom" of walking through a heavily booby-trapped area in the dark.

No sooner did we begin to move forward in the darkness than the first explosion occurred. The acting 2nd Platoon commander had tripped a booby trap, which critically wounded him and several others around him. The company commander went forward with the senior corpsman to assess the situation and help the wounded. A minute or two later a second explosion occurred. Word came back that the company commander had tripped a booby trap, which critically wounded him, the senior corpsman, and several others around them. (A rumor later circulated that the company commander had actually been "fragged"—assaulted with a fragmentation grenade—by a distraught member of the 2nd Platoon.) Bravo Company was "decapitated" of leadership and in disarray in the middle of a booby-trapped area in the dark. Then it began to rain.

We gathered the casualties, walking as gingerly as we could, and established a half-assed perimeter. We called for a medevac chopper but were told they were no longer flying because of bad weather. We explained that our company commander was an "emergency" medevac—meaning he would die if not evacuated quickly—so they agreed to divert a CH-46 Chinook helicopter that was returning to An Hoa with a badly wounded ARVN captain. About ten minutes later, the Chinook came in hard and landed fast. It dropped its rear ramp, and we began loading our casualties. After a couple of minutes, an enemy machine gun opened up from the direction of the village we had walked through earlier, instantly killing the chopper pilot and the wounded ARVN captain. The copilot panicked and immediately took off, nose up and ramp down. Two of our guys who had been carrying our casualties on board slid out the back of the chopper and hung by their fingers from the lowered ramp. At about an altitude of thirty feet, the first let go and fell into an adjacent rice paddy. At about fifty or sixty feet, the second let go and plummeted into the same rice paddy. The chopper quickly flew off, leaving us with two more casualties and no way of evacuating them.

We stayed up all night waiting for a further attack and too afraid of booby traps to move. The next morning, we carried our casualties in ponchos back through the village and back up the hill. We then had another medevac chopper fly out our "fallen" comrades. We remained the rest of the day and that night on the small hill and went north the next day. After we traveled about a half mile, the acting company commander looked back at the hill we had just left and spotted through his binoculars what he said were VC guerrillas rummaging through our abandoned position. I looked through his binoculars and saw only children, probably from that village at the bottom of the reverse slope of the hill. He told me to call in an artillery mission on the position. I balked, because they clearly looked like children to me. He disagreed and again ordered me to call in the artillery mission. I complied and obliterated the position using two batteries of artillery, one walking the rounds up the forward slope of the hill and the other walking the rounds up the reverse slope, where the village was.

Late that night, while sleeping in the mud and rain at our next position, I was bitten in the throat by a giant poisonous centipede. Fiery pain immediately began to move through my left shoulder and down my left arm. The acting senior corpsman took me to the acting company commander to have me medevaced out. (One has lots of "acting" positions in a depleted unit.) The sleepy, exhausted commander, not realizing that I was standing outside his makeshift tent with the corpsman, told the corpsman that no choppers would fly in bad weather, but if I was still alive in the morning, he would get me out of there. (I was not amused.) The corpsman then took me back to my "tent"

The tent that I "shared" with a giant poisonous centipede (January 1969)

(two ponchos snapped together and staked down) and gave me a bunch of painkillers. As the pills began to take effect, I wondered if I would ever wake up again. But soon I didn't care. The next morning I awoke pain-free, with just a red welt at the base of my throat for my troubles.

In just the first two weeks of our four-week assignment in the Arizona Territory, we suffered more than 50 percent casualties, including our company commander, a platoon commander, two platoon sergeants, our senior corpsman, and our 81 mm mortar forward observer. (I was slightly wounded by a bomb fragment in one of those "friendly fire" incidents and remained with the company.) Bravo Company had to be pulled out of the field earlier than intended, because our company was so understrength it was no longer operational.

We all grew to hate the war and just wanted to go home alive. The "cause" for which we had been told we were fighting seemed too abstract to the average Vietnamese peasant. Our Vietnamese ally was far weaker than we had been led to believe, and our Vietnamese enemy was far stronger, far more numerous, and had far more popular support than we had been led to believe. To most of us the war was a "waste." During the thirteen months I was in Vietnam, the acronym UUUU (or U-4) began appearing on Marine helmets and flak jackets. It meant "We are the unwilling, led by the unqualified, to do the unnecessary, for the ungrateful." The popular advice for "winning" war was "First, put all the good gooks on barges off the coast of Vietnam. Then use our B-52s to bomb the entire country into rubble, cover it with asphalt, and make it the world's largest parking lot. Then sink all the barges, because the only good gook is a dead gook." (When you begin to take that attitude toward the very people you are there to "save," it might be time to go home.) We didn't refer to the people as "Vietnamese"; they were "gooks," "zips" (for zipper head), "slopes" (for sloped head), "dinks," and "slant eyes." "Luke the Gook" was the favored name for the enemy. And in a guerrilla war, all Vietnamese were potentially your enemy.

When we returned to our home base after the nightmare in the Arizona Territory, the artillery officer at COC asked me what he could do for me. I immediately replied: "I want out of the field!" I had lost most of my friends over the previous weeks, I had finally been wounded myself, and my nerves were shot. So I went back to the artillery battery until my thirteen months were up and it was time for me to rotate back to "the world."

First, the battery commander made me club sergeant, which meant I was to manage the Bam Boo Bar, a beer-and-soda club for the enlisted men. That lasted all of two weeks. I ran into the battery commander late one night. Neither of us was entirely sober, but I was a corporal and he was a lieutenant. He demanded the keys for the club and told me that he was going to send me back out with the grunts. The next morning, however, he put me in charge of the trash detail, and I managed to hold on to that job until I rotated home in late March 1969.

The Bam Boo Bar (February 1968)

Trash detail (March 1969)

ANTIWARRIOR

I returned from Vietnam a changed person. I wasn't spat on at the airport, nor did I see any antiwar demonstrators, but I did see plenty of Hare Krishnas. I no longer believed in the war, but I would not tolerate any nonveteran criticizing the war in my presence. I especially hated those snotty college kids running around university campuses waving Viet Cong flags.

The first crack in this edifice occurred when my conservative, Bill Buckley–loving older brother, Gerry, informed me that he was going to attend a national "moratorium" march against the war in Washington in November 1969. That gave me pause. My breaking point, however, came in the spring of 1970, when President Nixon ordered the invasion of Cambodia, and then the Ohio National Guard fired on student demonstrators at Kent State. I knew the truth about Vietnam and could not live with the lies any longer. Why we were in Vietnam was a lie, the "progress" we were making was a lie, the way we treated the Vietnamese was a lie, and the argument that we couldn't just "cut and run" was a lie. So I decided to join the one anti-war group I thought would really understand what I was going through: the Vietnam Veterans Against the War.

In joining VVAW, it was my great hope that we could stop a war built upon lies from killing any more Americans and any more Vietnamese. I also hoped that the United States could somehow learn the lessons that might prevent us from being tricked into any more bloody protracted quagmires. The Vietnam War finally ended several years and many thousands of unnecessary casualties later, and for three decades the United States managed to stay out of quagmires. But those who bitterly and mindlessly rejected the lessons of Vietnam have dusted off the old deceptions and have, once again, fooled the United States into a bloody, protracted, needless quagmire. To get out of the current quagmire in Iraq, and to do so faster and with fewer casualties than we did in Vietnam, we must first come to terms with how the quagmire process worked in Vietnam, and how it was eventually reversed.

Home from the 'Nam with Mom (March 1969)

THREE

THE VIETNAM QUAGMIRE

While the war hawks would rejoice when it began,
the people would weep before it ended.
—*Walter Lippmann*

The Vietnam War was a bad war. It divided the United States
more deeply and bitterly than any other national crisis since
the Civil War. It destroyed two presidents, polarized Congress,
paralyzed the courts, turned the university campuses and urban
streets into battlegrounds, divided families, and almost ruined
the U.S. Army. It was a bad time that is best not repeated. How
could such a debacle occur? How was this quagmire created
and maintained? The short and simple answer is through deception—massive, systematic, intentional, official deception.

The creators and sustainers of the quagmire in Vietnam were
men who spoke the language of idealistic values publicly, but
that of ruthless power, privately. As the leading realist scholar of
international relations, John Mearshiemer, explained:

Because Americans dislike realpolitik, public discourse about foreign policy in the United States is usually couched in the language

of liberalism. Hence the pronouncements of policy elites are heavily flavored with optimism and moralism.... Behind closed doors, however, the elites make national security policy speak mostly the language of power, not that of principle, and the United States acts in the international system according to the dictates of realist logic. In essence, a discernable gap separates public rhetoric from the actual conduct of American foreign policy.[1]

These political and military leaders theoretically subscribed to the post-1945 legal and moral international order that limited the use of national military power. However, they believed that the development of nuclear weapons so fundamentally changed international relations that, when defending against a threat to the U.S. position of primacy in the world, the normal international legal and moral limits to military power did not apply to the United States. These leaders were convinced that in places such as Vietnam, "the gloves must come off" and that the United States had to use dirty methods like the enemy, to fight fire with fire.

At the same time, these leaders recognized that they could not be honest and forthright when explaining to "naive" Americans the real reasons for the war and the real methods used to fight it. Therefore, in building and sustaining the Vietnam quagmire, these leaders used idealistic rhetoric, such as "winning hearts and minds," but actually promulgated realist policies, such as "Grab 'em by the balls, and their hearts and minds will follow!"[2] These U.S. leaders also assured the nation that U.S. troops would never torture prisoners or kill innocent civilians. However, they promulgated policies such as "search and destroy," "body count," "free fire zones," "harassment and interdiction fire," and "carpet bombing" that, in their extreme, led logically to "Kill them all, and let God sort them out!"[3]

U.S. political and military leaders deceived the nation about the reasons for going into Vietnam, the progress being made in the war, the methods being used to fight it, and the difficulties of withdrawing from Vietnam. The evidence for this great deception is available in the publications of the best scholars, journalists, and policy analysts on the war. It is also available in the Pentagon's own top-secret study of the war, the leaked *Pentagon Papers.* And it is finally available in top-secret Central Intelligence Agency and National Security Agency documents declassified during the past year—thirty years after the war's end (and in the middle of another quagmire in Iraq)! Together, this evidence amounts to a damning indictment of U.S. political and military leaders who assumed that dishonesty, deception, and illegality are the ways to lead the nation into a distant, bloody, unnecessary war.

ENTERING: DECEPTION ABOUT PURPOSE

From 1946 to 1950, the Truman administration covertly supplied the French government with advanced U.S. military equipment and helped transport this U.S. military equipment and French troops to Indochina for use against Ho Chi Minh's Viet Minh. Additionally, the United States was providing France with substantial financial support, without which France could not have fought its colonial war in Vietnam. But according to George McTurnan Kahin, one of the few Vietnam scholars in the early years of U.S. involvement, the Truman administration kept all of this important information from the American people and Congress. Instead, the Truman administration knowingly misled Congress and the nation into believing the myth that the U.S. government was *not* assisting the French in their reimposition of colonial rule in Vietnam.[4]

For their part, the French had no illusions about what they were trying to do in Vietnam. Paris did not share Washington's grand strategic concern about losing an important region of the world to Moscow in the "great game" of power politics. The French were primarily concerned about losing their colonial empire in Southeast Asia. For the overwhelming majority of Vietnamese, their overriding concern was finally winning independence from France. As another U.S. scholar of Vietnam, Ellen Hammer, saw it in 1955, "The only freedom that most Vietnamese wanted was not from communism, about which they knew little and understood less, but from France."[5] Thus, our leaders told us the first large lie to lure us into the quagmire.

The Truman administration was finally able to support, overtly, the French colonial war against the Vietnamese when North Korea invaded South Korea in June 1950. This was the pretext for which the Truman administration had been looking. In his request to Congress for funds to repel the North Korean invasion, President Truman included a request for aid to the French to fight Ho Chi Minh and the Viet Minh.[6] The outbreak of war in Korea enabled the Truman White House to repackage, virtually overnight, a French colonial war the U.S. people and Congress could not and did not support into an international anticommunist crusade the U.S. nation, in the midst of the McCarthy "red scare" years, could and did support. The second quagmire lie was successfully told.

From 1950 to 1954, both the Truman and Eisenhower administrations steadily increased U.S. military and financial assistance to the French. The United States was becoming more directly involved in other ways, as well. During the battle for Dien Bien Phu in the spring of 1954, U.S. CIA pilots secretly flew bombing missions in support of the beleaguered French forces. Meanwhile, in Washington, the Joint Chiefs of Staff seriously debated the wisdom of using tactical nuclear weapons against Viet Minh in the hills around Dien Bien Phu.[7] Top-secret CIA documents, finally released to the public more than half a century later, indicate that there remained, at the highest levels of U.S. government, serious consideration of the use of nuclear weapons against the Viet Minh after the fall of Dien Bien Phu. A CIA intelligence estimate from June 15, 1954, read, "Nuclear weapons would be employed if their use was deemed militarily advantageous, but nuclear attacks on the Indochinese civil population as a target system would be avoided."[8]

The next day, June 16, 1954 (after successful U.S. "inducement"), Vietnam's emperor, Bao Dai—the "nightclub emperor" living on the French Riviera—asked Ngo Dinh Diem to form a Vietnamese government in the south to oppose Ho Chi Minh and the Viet Minh.[9] Ngo Dinh Diem had briefly worked as Bao Dai's secretary in 1933 but quit because the French exerted decisive control over the emperor. When the French set up a phony "autonomous" Bao Dai government in February 1950, Diem left Vietnam in disgust and went into exile. Diem first went to Japan and then to the United States, where he lived in Maryknoll seminaries in New York and New Jersey. Meanwhile, Washington and London gave formal diplomatic recognition to the Bao Dai "government" and successfully encouraged other nations in the West to do the same. From 1950 to 1954, Diem, a devout Catholic, cultivated friends in high places, such as Cardinal Spellman and Senators Mike Mansfield and John Kennedy. Diem returned to Vietnam shortly after Bao Dai appointed him prime minister.

The fall of Dien Bien Phu to the Viet Minh in the spring of 1954 finally shattered the political will of the French people to continue to support the war in Indochina. So the French entered negotiations with the Viet Minh in Geneva. The talks eventually produced the Geneva Accords of 1954, which stipulated that Vietnam be temporarily divided along the 17th parallel for a period of two years, after which free elections were to be held to reunite the country under one government. Viet Minh forces were to withdraw to the northern half, and the French forces were to withdraw to the southern half. However, the Eisenhower administration, fearing that Ho Chi Minh and the Viet Minh would win free elections if they were held in 1956, instead decided to avoid democratic elections and create, virtually out of thin air, a new country in the south called the Republic of Viet Nam (RVN). This historical deception was officially confirmed by a recently declassified 1954 CIA report, which stated, "If the scheduled national elections are held in July 1956, and if the Viet Minh does not prejudice its political prospects, the Viet Minh will almost certainly win."[10]

The United States, with a CIA team led by Colonel Edward Lansdale, supported, funded, and guided Diem's brutal and dictatorial consolidation of power in the south.[11] Diem, in the name of "democratic anticommunism," canceled the democratic elections, mandated by the Geneva Accords and scheduled for 1956, and launched a campaign of bribery or violent repression against all possible political rivals in the south, communist and noncommunist.[12] Of course the U.S. people were told none of this at the time. The path into the great Vietnam quagmire was steadily being paved with more and more deception.

Ngo Dinh Diem was personally "clean," but his government, run by close family members such as his brother, Ngo Dinh Nhu, was repressive, corrupt, and brutal. The U.S.-created South Vietnamese military—the Army of the Republic of Vietnam (ARVN)—was, with rare exception, cowardly and unwilling to fight the tough, highly motivated Viet Cong (VC) guerrillas. David Halberstam, as a young journalist in Vietnam, saw clear evidence of this while traveling in the field with the ARVN and their U.S. military advisers. He and the U.S. military advisers involved in the battle were astounded that U.S. political and military leaders in Saigon, who wanted only good news to appear in U.S. newspapers back home, repackaged the disastrous January 1963 battle of Ap Bac into a "great success." As Halberstam wrote at the time, "having suffered a stunning defeat, the American military headquarters referred to it as a victory."[13] Neil Sheehan, the biographer of Colonel John Paul Vann, the senior U.S. adviser at Ap Bac, devotes an entire section of his Pulitzer prize-winning book, *A Bright Shining Lie*, to the battle and the subsequent massive deception and calumny of U.S. political and military leaders in the wake of Ap Bac.[14]

ARVN incompetence, combined with Diem's growing defiance of the increasing Americanization of the war, contributed to the strengthening of the Viet Cong, the paralysis of the Saigon government, and Washington's decision in late 1963 to get rid of Diem. The United States had put Diem in power; the United States could take him out. A coterie of U.S.-friendly ARVN generals, with CIA direction and support, overthrew Diem and killed him and his brother in a coup on November 2, 1963. Lt. Colonel Lucien Conein, the CIA's top agent in South Vietnam, served as adviser, supplier, and go-between to the generals. Ellen Hammer described the scene at the coup generals' headquarters on the day of the coup:

> [General Don] found Lucien Conein already installed there, with a direct telephone line to the American Embassy. Don had sent word to him during the morning that the generals were about to act and needed the money he had on hand. "In case we fail, you're going with us," General Minh told Conein when he arrived.
>
> The American had brought three million piastres and a radio that cut him into a special network so that he was in touch with the CIA station and with other CIA officers. Thus, Conein stayed in communication with Washington by telephone and radio, as he had been from the beginning, ever since he had first become involved with the coup.[15]

These crucial facts, too, were kept from the U.S. public. Instead, U.S. officials claimed with a straight face that the United States had nothing to do with the coup.

For the next year to eighteen months, the United States sought Vietnamese military leaders competent enough to govern Vietnam under Washington's guidance. Failing this, the United States decided to take direct control of the war. Therefore, the Johnson administration manufactured the Gulf of Tonkin "incidents" in order to rally the American people to support direct U.S. military intervention in Vietnam. U.S./ARVN Special Forces conducting covert raids along the coast of North Vietnam provoked the first attack by North Vietnamese patrol boats on the U.S. destroyer *Maddox*. The U.S. National Security Agency (NSA) then concocted the second "attack" against the *Maddox* and the *Turner Joy*. These facts were not officially admitted until more than thirty years later.[16]

Between August 1964 and March 1965, the Johnson administration launched a massive bombing campaign against North Vietnam and sent the first major U.S. ground combat forces into Vietnam. Lyndon Johnson and his civilian advisers deceived the American people into believing that these steps were intended to avoid a larger war, and the Joint Chiefs of Staff went along with the deception rather than risk their careers.[17] Indeed, the history of how the United States entered the Vietnam quagmire reveals a pattern of systematic governmental lying to the American people, precisely those who would have to pay the bill for the war in "blood and treasure."

SINKING DEEPER: DECEPTION ABOUT PROGRESS

From 1965, when the first U.S. combat units entered Vietnam, until the Tet Offensive of 1968, when the credibility of the U.S. government finally collapsed, U.S. civilian and military leaders in Saigon and Washington insisted that "progress" in the war was being made. Lost battles were magically turned into "victories" by U.S. Military Assistance Command, Vietnam (MACV), General Westmoreland's headquarters in Saigon. David Maraniss, in his recently published book, *They Marched into Sunlight*, gives us a good example of Westmoreland's insidious deception regarding U.S. "progress" being made in the war. In October 1967, the Viet Cong's 1st Regiment ambushed and decimated elements of 2/28, the "Black Lions" battalion of the 1st Infantry Division, the U.S. Army's famed "Big Red One," northwest of Saigon. There was absolutely no doubt among the U.S. soldiers who survived the slaughter that it was a terrible defeat for the United States. In fact, one survivor likened it to Custer's last stand at the Little Big Horn. However, as Maraniss explained: "At Westmoreland's direction, his aides kept massaging the story, pressing the argument that the battle was a victory."[18]

Even more despicable was the numbers deception Westmoreland was playing at MACV in Saigon. Since a "body count" of the enemy killed was the chief way Secretary of Defense Robert McNamara and General Westmoreland measured progress in the war, daily, weekly, and monthly body count figures were issued by MACV, the Pentagon, and the White House as evidence of their "winning" strategy. The goal of this strategy of "attrition" was to kill the enemy faster than they could be replaced. Theoretically, when this was accomplished, the "crossover point" was achieved and Westmoreland, McNamara, and Lyndon Johnson could claim the United States was winning the war.

However, to achieve this "crossover point" on paper, Westmoreland needed to reduce the total enemy strength to below their replacement numbers. He accomplished this largely by dropping an entire category of the enemy called "irregular VC." He ordered this done, explaining that they were no real threat to U.S. troops, despite the Pentagon's own data showing that these local guerrillas had been responsible for setting the mines and booby traps that caused approximately 37 percent of all U.S. casualties in Vietnam during the previous year.[19] General Westmoreland was pressured to do this by Chairman of the Joint Chiefs of Staff General Earle Wheeler, who in turn was pressured by President Lyndon Johnson, who was facing a tough reelection campaign in the coming year. The Central Intelligence Agency, however, knew better and all but lost a bitter bureaucratic battle with the Pentagon—which had decisive White House backing—to keep this critical category of enemy in the total estimate. In the end, the CIA grudgingly became an accomplice in MACV's conspiracy to fix the intelligence to White House politics and adjusted its November 13, 1967, intelligence estimate to reflect Westmoreland's phony lower enemy numbers.[20] The following is an excerpt from this only recently declassified document:

> Though the aggregate numbers on these groups [self-defense, secret self-defense, "Assault Youth," etc.] are still large and constitute a part of the overall Communist effort, they are not offensive military forces. Hence, they are not included in the military order of battle total.... We conclude that the strength of the Communist military forces and political organizations in South Vietnam declined in the last year.... We believe that there is a fairly good chance that the overall strength and effectiveness of the military forces and the political infrastructure will continue to decline.[21]

Eight days after this phony intelligence estimate was issued, Westmoreland made his "light at the end of the tunnel" speech at the National Press Club in Washington, D.C. LBJ brought

"Westy" back home to shore up Johnson's sagging polling numbers on the war, which had been sliding badly. This was the White House's all-out "Success Offensive" to convince the American people that their fears and doubts about progress in the war were misplaced. General Westmoreland assured the nation that "we have reached an important point when the end begins to come into view." He asserted that the U.S. forces in Vietnam had reached that long-sought-after "crossover point" and that he could see "light at the end of the tunnel."[22] Five weeks later, Westy's "light at the end of the tunnel" turned out to be an oncoming train for those vulnerable U.S. troops attacked in the Tet Offensive.

The sham nature of the numbers game could not be hidden forever from LBJ's "wise men," whom he periodically trotted out before the media to show establishment support for his war. Dean Acheson, secretary of state under President Truman during the Korean War, finally got fed up with the phony numbers being presented to him. He realized that the numbers were "either false or incomplete." In the immediate wake of the Tet Offensive, in the basement of the White House during one of Johnson's infamous tirades on the war, Acheson quietly got up and walked out of the White House and across Lafayette Park to his law office in the Union Trust Building. "The phone rang immediately; it was Walt Rostow [Johnson's national security adviser] asking why he had walked out. 'You tell the President— and you tell him precisely in these words,' Acheson said evenly, 'that he can take Vietnam and stick it up his ass.'"[23]

HITTING BOTTOM: DECEPTION ABOUT METHODS

U.S. leaders also lied when they claimed that the United States was using legally appropriate methods in fighting the war, and they further lied when they claimed that uncovered U.S. war crimes were "aberrations" perpetrated by "a few bad apples" at the lowest end of the chain of command. The truth is that many of the U.S. military's methods for fighting the war—which were promulgated by their civilian leaders back in Washington—were inherently illegal and immoral. As Telford Taylor, U.S. chief prosecutor at the Nuremberg Trials, explained regarding the widespread U.S. practice of destruction of villages for punitive purposes: "It is clear that such reprisal attacks are a flagrant violation of the Geneva Convention on Civilian Protection, which prohibits 'collective penalties' and 'reprisals against protected persons,' and equally in violation of the Rules of Land Warfare."[24]

The torturing of prisoners and detainees to elicit intelligence was another fairly common U.S. activity in Vietnam. The use of fists, knives, pistols, and rifle butts during the interrogation of VCS (Viet Cong suspects) is well documented.[25] Also common was the use of water torture, electrical torture, and tossing bound prisoners from airborne helicopters. K. Barton Osborn, an Army intelligence specialist in Vietnam in 1967–1968, described in a 1970 public hearing in Washington the "half-a-chopper-ride" technique of interrogation:

> I went along twice when they would go up in helicopters, which belonged to the Marine Division and take two detainees along. They used one as a scare mechanism for the other. If they wanted to interrogate Detainee A, they would take someone along who was either in bad health or whom they had already written off as a loss—take both these Vietnamese along in the helicopter and they would say, they would start investigating Detainee B, the one they had no interest in, and they wouldn't get any information out of him and so they would threaten to throw him out of the helicopter. All the time, of course, the detainee they wanted information from was watching. And they would threaten and threaten and, finally, they would throw him out of the helicopter. I was there when this happened twice and it was very effective, because, of course, at the time step one was to throw the person out of the helicopter and step two was to say, "You're next." And that quite often broke them down, demoralized them, and at that point they would give whatever information.[26]

Another favored technique of extracting information from detainees was the use of a TA-312 field telephone. The telephone's bared wires (often "copper green" from the damp tropical air) were attached to the most sensitive body parts of a naked male or female detainee. When the interrogator received an answer he didn't like, or got no answer at all, he would turn the crank handle of the phone, which would generate an electrical current approximately equivalent to an automobile battery, thus making the detainee jump and scream in pain. This technique was nicknamed "The Bell Telephone Hour," after a popular weekly television show during the 1950s.[27]

Some U.S. interrogators got quite creative in their use of torture in Vietnam. Steve Noetzel, a Green Beret sergeant with 5th Special Forces in Vietnam in 1963–1964, described one of these methods:

> At the B Team in Can Tho ... they had an eight-foot python snake, which was kept at the camp in a cage, supposedly for rat control. When we had prisoners or detainees who were brought to the B Team, they were immediately questioned, and if they balked at all or sounded like they weren't going to be cooperative, they were simply placed in a room overnight.... The door was locked, and this snake was thrown in there with them. Now the python is a constrictor, similar to a boa. It's not poisonous. It will snap at you but it's not poisonous, and it probably can't kill a full-grown American or a large male, but it sure terrified the Vietnamese. Two of them usually in a room overnight with the python snake, struggling with it most of the night, I guess, and we could hear them screaming. In fact, on one instance, they had to go in there and gag the prisoners, so they wouldn't keep everyone awake all night. In the morning they were usually more cooperative.[28]

While it is true that most U.S. troops in Vietnam neither witnessed nor participated in any war crimes, it is just as true that most U.S. troops were not "in the bush" in ground combat units, and so most had no opportunity to acquire firsthand knowledge of U.S. atrocities. The "tail-to-tooth ration" in Vietnam was 6:1, meaning that only 15 percent of all U.S. troops in Vietnam were in sustained combat. Most U.S. troops were in support units as truck drivers, dental assistants, airplane mechanics, and office clerks. They only heard the rumors of atrocities, which were persistent. Far right critics of Vietnam war crime allegations assert that many of the Vietnam veterans who described U.S. war crimes after their return from Vietnam were "frauds" who never served in Vietnam and fabricated their allegations. Specifically, B. G. Burkett and Glenna Whitley's book, *Stolen Valor,* and Carleton Sherwood's documentary film, *Stolen Honor,* make this accusation.[29] And both rely entirely on the same single source, Guenter Lewy's *America in Vietnam.*[30] Lewy claimed that a number of "fake" witnesses appeared at the Winter Soldier Investigation (WSI), and therefore the credibility of the entire three days of testimony is suspect.[31] However, the Pentagon never publicly challenged the authenticity of the witnesses at WSI (all of whom brought their military discharge papers to Detroit), and to this day, Lewy has not been able to produce the "evidence" he claimed he had of "fake" witnesses.[32]

U.S. violations of the laws of war were fairly routine in the bush, such as the Americal Division's infamous massacre of more than 500 unarmed Vietnamese civilians in the hamlet of My Lai in March 1968.[33] Additional U.S. atrocities, usually on a smaller scale than My Lai, were later discovered and continue to be uncovered three decades after the Vietnam War ended.[34] Whenever such atrocities were discovered, U.S. civilian and military leaders usually avoided their command responsibility by shifting the blame to those in the lower ranks. Telford Taylor wrote of the challenge of establishing command responsibility in the confusion of an insurgency: "For the lower ranks, these [difficult] circumstances must count powerfully in mitigation of their culpability. But in these confused, complex, and shifting circumstances, the responsibility of the highest officers for training, doctrine and practice is all the greater."[35]

A few revisionist historians have described the Tet Offensive of 1968 as a major U.S. "victory." These historians usually insist that the Viet Cong spearheaded the Tet Offensive and were largely destroyed by withering U.S. firepower. They complain that just as we had the enemy on the ropes, the United States capitulated and Washington decided to negotiate, while gradually withdrawing U.S. troops from Vietnam. According to this version of reality, the United States forfeited politically what it had just "won" militarily. However, the cold facts belie this wishful scenario. The Defense Department's own records show that the United States suffered its highest casualties of the war not in the year *preceding* the 1968 Tet Offensive, but in the year *following* the Tet Offensive, when the Viet Cong were supposedly decimated by Tet and "on the ropes."[36] Indeed, I can personally attest to the fact that the VC were highly active and effective in areas southwest of Da Nang between August 1968 and March 1969, sniping, triggering ambushes, and setting booby traps that maimed and killed so many of the Marines and Navy corpsmen around me. (See chapter 2.)

The shock of the Tet Offensive in early 1968 and the revelations in late 1969 of the My Lai massacre, combined with the rising U.S. death toll, triggered the collapse of domestic public support for the war. The costs of the war had finally outstripped the American people's faith in its purpose and progress. The war was killing young American men by the tens of thousands, killing innocent Vietnamese civilians by the hundreds of thousands, weakening the U.S. economy, and bitterly dividing U.S. society as nothing had since the Civil War. And the war just kept dragging on and on with no end in sight. For what good purpose were our troops continuing to die? To stop the Kremlin's "world communist conspiracy," when Washington was busy dancing "détente" with Moscow?[37] To save "democracy" in South Vietnam when our Vietnamese allies in Saigon were rigging elections, jailing their political opponents, stealing U.S. economic assistance, and making millions from the illegal heroin trade?[38] To achieve "peace with honor"? With the collapse of U.S. public support for the war, the media, Congress, political parties, and interest groups began turning against the war with enthusiasm.

Antiwar demonstrations became larger and more frequent, and U.S. voters began registering their growing displeasure with the war in the voting booth. Domestic support for the war was hitting rock bottom.[39]

Meanwhile, in Vietnam, the U.S. military—mainly the Army and the Marines, who bore the chief burden of fighting the war on the ground—was rapidly disintegrating. The Vietnam quagmire was destroying the military as a viable U.S. institution. Studies showed that, by 1971, 50.9 percent of all U.S. troops in Vietnam were smoking marijuana and 28.5 percent were using heroin occasionally or regularly. The heaviest drug use was among combat units, rendering them inoperable.[40] Search-and-destroy missions were turned into "search-and-evade," and cases of outright mutiny among U.S. units in the field mushroomed. In October 1971, for example, a platoon from the 1st Air Cavalry Division refused to go out on a dangerous night ambush. They were replaced with another platoon, which also refused. Sixty-five men from the company, including nine sergeants, signed a petition stating that they preferred to be brought up on charges rather than carry out an order they considered "suicidal."[41]

Most mutinies in U.S. units ended in compromise rather than harsh disciplinary action, because commanders feared being "fragged" in the night. "Fragging" was the assassination of one's commander, usually with a fragmentation grenade. The grunts preferred grenades over rifles or pistols, because grenades left little forensic evidence. Department of Defense figures indicate that fragging incidents increased in frequency from ninety-six in 1969 to well over two hundred in 1971. Congressional estimates put the fragging numbers at well over a thousand, although the actual numbers could be even higher.[42] Marine Colonel William Corson described fraggings as "a servicewide game of psychological warfare on the part of enlisted men against their superior officers and NCOs." General Bruce Palmer wrote that fragging incidents "were literally murderous indications of poor morale and became a matter of deep concern."[43] General Palmer obviously had a flair for understatement.

Desertion rates in both the Army and the Marine Corps shot up, reenlistments dropped, and an increasing number of officers resigned their commissions during this difficult period. Thirty-eight ROTC units were expelled from college campuses, and five hundred assaults occurred upon ROTC facilities nationwide. Surviving ROTC programs experienced drastic reductions in enrollment.[44] Outright political resistance to the war within the military became widespread in Vietnam, at home, and at U.S. bases in Germany and Japan. There were at least 14 dissident GI organizations, 11 off-base coffeehouses, and 144 underground GI newspapers.[45] The spray-painted initials FTA began appearing on and off Army posts around the world. Dissident GIs transformed what had been the Army's favorite recruiting slogan of "Fun, Travel, and Adventure!" into "Fuck the Army!" Jane Fonda, Donald Sutherland, and a cast of antiwar performers headed up a world-traveling entertainment show—intended as an alternative to the war-supporting Bob Hope show—that they called "The FTA Show."[46]

In 1971, Marine Colonel Robert Heinl summed up the accumulated impact of all these indicators of breakdown within the U.S. military:

> The morale, discipline and battleworthiness of the U.S. armed forces are, with a few salient exceptions, lower and worse than at any time in this century and possibly in the history of the United States. By every conceivable indicator, our army that now remains in Vietnam is in a state approaching collapse, with individual units avoiding and having refused combat, murdering their officers and noncommissioned officers, drug-ridden and dispirited where not near-mutinous.[47]

Without an effective Army, the U.S. war in Vietnam was impossible to sustain. (For those who would later argue that we could have "won" the Vietnam War with more patience and political support, I must ask, "With what army?") It was time to get out of Vietnam. Lawrence Korb, a defense analyst and an official in the Pentagon during the Reagan administration, addressed the tragic irony of the situation: "Many observers noted poignantly that in the early 1960s the United States placed the military in Vietnam to save that nation, but by the late 1960s our forces had to be taken out in order to save the military."[48]

BLOCKING THE EXIT: DECEPTION ABOUT THE DIFFICULTY OF WITHDRAWAL

Leaders in Washington were disingenuous when they claimed that withdrawing from Vietnam would make the plight of the Vietnamese much worse and would make Americans look like "cut-and-run cowards." The truth is that the Vietnamese are today better off living in a united, independent country at peace, and the United States is better off having ended the massive killing, rejuvenated its economy, rebuilt its Army, and restored its reputation in the world.

The Nixon administration, however, argued that rapid withdrawal would mean abandoning our "noble ally"—an ally Nixon's own defense secretary, Melvin Laird, decades later would admit was "corrupt, selfish men who were no more than dictators in the garb of statesmen."[49] Instead, the Nixon administration demanded "peace with honor" and chose to obstruct the U.S. exit from Vietnam with a phony "Vietnamization" program. This program was a fraud from the start. It was sold to the American people and Congress as a way of withdrawing, slowly, U.S. ground troops and replacing them with ARVN units capable of fighting on their own. In reality, what the United States got was a much wider war, a secret, illegal bombing campaign in Cambodia, continuing U.S. casualties, and an ARVN that was more dependent than ever on U.S. money and firepower, albeit from U.S. air and naval power.

The Nixon administration was able to drag out U.S. involvement in the Vietnam War for five more years by deceiving the American people and attacking the war's critics through a systematic process of unlawful activity. Nixon's White House operators believed that "national security" made them exempt from the law. The Nixon White House rejected the constitutional balance of power and the roles of Congress and the courts. It tapped phones without court orders. It sent teams of ex-CIA agents to burglarize the homes and offices of its antiwar critics, looking for evidence of alleged "foreign" connections.[50] (In 1971, my apartment at 44th and Spruce in West Philly was burglarized a short time after I returned from a VVAW-sponsored antiwar trip through Europe. The "burglars" painstakingly went through all of my papers and photos from the trip but somehow "missed" some cash I kept in the top drawer of my bureau.)

This imperial presidential system of "spectacular and historic illegality" led directly to the Watergate burglary. And the Nixon White House would have gotten away with it if not for a low-paid security guard in the Watergate, who found a piece of tape over a door lock and reported it. Walter Lippmann, the dean of Washington journalists, summed up the real threat such actions present to our constitutional democracy: "Watergate shows how very *vulnerable* our constitutional system is. If the national government falls into the hands of sufficiently unprincipled and unscrupulous men, they can do terrible things before anyone can stop them."[51]

Political leaders can claim that they are fighting a distant, bloody, open-ended war for "freedom, democracy, and the rule of law." But if the government that they are "supporting" is in fact corrupt, repressive, brutal, and completely dependent on U.S. lives and money to keep it going, then our leaders have sold us a bill of goods. And if, at the same time our leaders are preaching "freedom, democracy, and the rule of law" overseas while doing their best to subvert it at home, then our leaders are liars, hypocrites, and criminals.

In the final analysis, the war in Vietnam was never really about helping the Vietnamese. U.S. political and military leaders from the Truman administration to the Nixon administration were primarily concerned about beating the other superpower, the Soviet Union, in the "great game" of power politics. It was about enforcing U.S. control over the region of Southeast Asia and establishing U.S. hegemony in the world as a whole. The United States did finally pull out of Vietnam, with the help of "alternative" leaders in the antiwar movement, the GI movement, and the Vietnam veterans' movement. But this occurred *despite* the dishonest, illegal, and immoral rear-guard stalling actions of U.S. leaders and only after thoroughly devastating Vietnam and completely traumatizing the United States.

In the wake of the Vietnam War, learning lessons from this national tragedy became a survival imperative for the United States. Applying these lessons, and applying them well, became the United States' only hope of preventing unprincipled and unscrupulous political and military leaders from doing this to the United States all over again, somewhere else, in some future decade.

Author's first visit to the Vietnam War Memorial in Washington, D.C. (1990)

FOUR

⸙

THE LESSONS OF VIETNAM

... war crimes without criminals, lies without liars,
a process of immaculate deception.
—*Daniel Ellsberg*

Some have said that we failed to learn the lessons of Vietnam. This is not quite true. The United States did, in fact, learn lessons from Vietnam. The problem is we learned *too many* lessons, and they frequently contradict each other. This occurred because the Vietnam War was so bitterly divisive and traumatic for the United States—and because the nation had argued so long and hard over it and consensus seemed impossible—that when the war finally did come to an end, the nation "agreed to disagree" and moved on. Hence, there are many different "lessons of Vietnam" but no national consensus, other than it was a very bad experience. For a university professor and Vietnam veteran like myself, this has made teaching a university honors program course on "The Lessons of Vietnam"—as I have for the past seventeen years—a bit of a "challenge."

Because there is always the danger that we will repeat our past mistakes if we do not learn from them, it has been especially important to teach the post-Vietnam generation about the war. However, the overwhelming majority of incoming freshmen over the past two decades know little or nothing about Vietnam, because their high school teachers avoided teaching it and their parents avoided talking about it, largely because Vietnam continues to be a raw scar on the Vietnam generation. Hence, year after year, the kids coming into college have an intense hunger to learn "the big secret" about what so divided the nation and traumatized their parents, but a secret kept from them to protect them from its ugliness. So I must teach them the ugliness of Vietnam … without indoctrinating them in my personal biases.

THE FIVE SCHOOLS

The way I have gone about this has been to classify the lessons of Vietnam into five "schools of thought," and over the years, I have developed a scheme based on cause, reason for failure, lesson, and personification (see table 4.1). These schools are, in their chronological order of development, Conservative, Liberal, Far Left, Far Right, and the Military.

The Conservative School on the lessons of Vietnam (late 1960s, early 1970s) held that the U.S. military intervention in Vietnam was fundamentally motivated by good intentions; that is, the desire to oppose communist tyranny and assist the Vietnamese people in their hour of need. The proponents of this school believed that the United States failed to achieve its goals in Vietnam because good, well-intentioned men made honest mistakes in judgment regarding the nature of the enemy and the limits of U.S. military power. The principal lesson the Conservative School learned from the Vietnam debacle was the necessity of appreciating the limits of any nation's power—even a military *super*power such as the United States—to control the course of world events. The Conservative School is best personified in former secretary of defense Robert S. McNamara.[1]

Table 4.1. Schools of Thought on the Lessons of Vietnam

School	Cause	Failing	Lesson	Personification
Conservative	Good intentions	Honest mistakes	Limits of power	Robert McNamara
Liberal	Imperial dominance	Illegal, immoral, deceptive policies	Importance of international law, morality, and democracy	Daniel Ellsberg
Far Left	Capitalism	Socialist resistance	Overthrow capitalism	Noam Chomsky
Far Right	Noble	Stabbed in the back	Redouble brute force	Richard Nixon
Military	Honorable	Forgot Clausewitz	A People's Army	Colin Powell

The Liberal School (late 1960s, early 1970s) posited that the real purpose behind the U.S. war on Vietnam was the classic imperial desire to control an important region of the world in the "great game" of international power politics. This school believed that the United States failed in Vietnam because the illegal, immoral, and deceptive policies U.S. leaders promulgated in Vietnam undermined core U.S. values and drained U.S. domestic political will to sustain the war in the face of ever-mounting losses. The central lesson for the Liberal School was the continuing relevance of law, democracy, morality, and personal responsibility. The individual who best personified the Liberal School on the lessons of Vietnam is Daniel Ellsberg.[2]

The Far Left School (late 1960s, early 1970s) contended that the underlying cause for U.S. intervention in Vietnam was the insatiable hunger of corporate capitalists for higher profits. Far Left critics of the war argued that U.S. foreign policy in Vietnam, although allegedly "democratic," actually served U.S. corporate capitalists' interest in accessing cheap foreign labor, cheap raw materials, new customers for U.S. products, and new areas for U.S. investment. For the proponents of this school, not just individual U.S. leaders were to blame for the disastrous war in Vietnam, but the entire U.S. capitalist system was at fault. The Far Left School explained that the United States failed in Vietnam because the Vietnamese people, aided by anticapitalist forces around the world, were more determined to prevail than the U.S. corporate elites and their political and military henchmen in Washington. For the Far Left School, the main lesson to be learned from Vietnam was that poor people around the world, if united, will never be defeated by the greedy, warmongering capitalists. The individual most commonly identified with this school is Noam Chomsky.[3]

The Far Right School on the lessons of Vietnam (late 1970s, early 1980s) believed that the U.S. war in Vietnam was a "noble cause" driven by the most altruistic motives: *freedom* for the Vietnamese people. The proponents of this school, unrepentant Cold Warriors and embryonic neoconservatives (neocons), insisted that the Vietnam War could have been won if the troops had been allowed to use unrestricted U.S. military power. They accused the liberal media, the spineless U.S. Congress, and the traitorous antiwar movement of betraying U.S. troops in Vietnam, of "stabbing them in the back." The central lesson they took from Vietnam was that the next time the United States goes to war, the U.S. must ignore international legal and moral "restrictions" and apply the full extent of superior U.S. military power, in addition to using the full extent of U.S. governmental power to suppress domestic critics. The Far Right School is best personified by President Richard Nixon.[4]

Finally, the Military School on the lessons of Vietnam (early to mid-1980s) held that the initial purpose of the war was honorable; that is, the military was just obeying lawful orders from its commander-in-chief in loyal service to its country. However, proponents of the Military School concluded that the war was lost because both senior civilian and military leaders made fatal strategic errors. They contended that senior military leaders failed to apply the basic principles of warfare propounded by Carl von Clausewitz a century and a half earlier and senior civilian leaders failed to rally the nation to support the Vietnam War. Therefore, the Military School concluded that U.S. military and civilian leaders must never again forget the vital strategic relationship between military force and domestic political support in initiating, sustaining, and winning a distant, bloody war. The personification of the Military School on the lessons of Vietnam is General Colin Powell.[5]

These categories are not perfect, and in fact there are some gray areas between two or three of these schools. Nevertheless, it doesn't take a rocket scientist to see some of the substantial differences between several of these schools of thought. They cannot all be reconciled. The Vietnam War could not have been both a noble cause *and* an immoral crime, an impossible adventure *and* a squandered victory, a mistake of using too much force *and* not using enough force. In the end, I give my students my own view, a fusion of the Conservative, Liberal, and

Military Schools, but I urge them to use their own independent judgment to decide in which school or schools they are most comfortable.

Outside of the classroom, the three schools closer to the mainstream and away from the Left and Right fringes—the Conservative, Liberal, and Military schools—have seen their lessons pushed to the forefront of U.S. society by two U.S. institutions trying to recover from organizational trauma sustained at the hands of the "imperial presidency" during the Vietnam War: Congress and the Army. Gradually, the lessons of the three central schools formed the unofficial consensus of U.S. lessons of Vietnam, and for three decades successfully prevented the nation from being dragged into any new Vietnam-like quagmires.

INSTITUTIONAL PREVENTION

The U.S. Congress, punished seat by seat by an electorate fed up with the war and government deception (not unlike in the 2006 midterm election), finally stood on its hind legs and reined in the "imperial presidency." It did so by passing—over presidential vetoes—the War Powers Resolution of 1973 and the Intelligence Act of 1976. The first piece of legislation forced the Executive Branch to secure legal authorization from the Legislative Branch for waging wars that last more than ninety days. Every president since 1973 has denied the constitutional need to get this congressional authorization, but no wars have been fought past ninety days without such authorization, in the form of a congressional resolution (e.g., Lebanon in 1982, Iraq in 1991, and Somalia in 1992).

The second piece of legislation created the House and Senate Select Committees on Intelligence, which have helped maintain legislative oversight on the covert games that presidents like to play in foreign affairs (e.g., the Iran-Contra scandal).

A few years after the high point of Congress's "reassertion" of its constitutional prerogatives regarding the war power, the

U.S. Army decided to study, learn, articulate, and disseminate its own lessons of Vietnam. The Army's lessons took the form of the "Weinberger Doctrine"—later to morph into the "Powell Doctrine"—that Secretary of Defense Caspar Weinberger announced in late 1984 (over the strenuous objections of Secretary of State George Shultz and the neoconservatives—neocons—in the Reagan administration). On November 28, 1984, Caspar Weinberger gave a speech in Washington during which he outlined six conditions for the proper use of force. These conditions are:

1. U.S. vital interests must be at stake.
2. A clear commitment must be made to victory.
3. The political and military objectives must be made clear.
4. Military forces must be properly sized.
5. Public and congressional support must be secured.
6. Force must be the last resort.[6]

These conditions were quickly endorsed by all four military services, and they expressed the collective wisdom of the top generals and admirals in the U.S. military regarding their bitter experiences in Vietnam.

The driving force behind the Weinberger Doctrine was the severe organizational damage experienced by the military as a whole—and the Army in particular—as a result of the Vietnam War. As noted in the previous chapter, the U.S. Army had experienced the organizational equivalent of a "near-death experience" in Vietnam, and its survivors vowed never again to let it happen to their beloved institution.[7]

Since these institutional constraints on the imperial presidency were promulgated, many academics, analysts, and pundits have spilled much ink debating their wisdom and effectiveness. Some say the War Powers Resolution (WPR) is impotent, allowing presidents to send forces into combat anywhere, anytime, for whatever reason. Others argue that the WPR has gone too far and that an "imperial Congress" has tied the hands of presidents too tightly in foreign affairs. In regard to the Weinberger-Powell Doctrine (W-PD), some argue that it indicates the generals *over-learned* the lessons of Vietnam and have become too afraid to use force, whereas others insist the W-PD forces presidents to consider critical strategic factors that would otherwise be left out.

Despite this lack of consensus, the most important point is that the War Powers Resolution and the Weinberger-Powell Doctrine were both intended to act as institutional constraints on the presidency's imperial temptation to drag the United States, yet again, into a distant, ambiguous, bloody quagmire. And fortunately, these formal institutional constraints had assistance from several other sources in the U.S. political system.

THE "VIETNAM SYNDROME"

Scholars, policy analysts, and policy makers have learned a couple of additional crucial lessons that have barely registered on the public's radar screen and remain buried deep in the academic literature. These lessons have, in the wake of Vietnam, become very important to those most concerned about the political process of taking the nation to war. The first of these lessons, revealed in John Mueller's now-classic *War, Presidents, and Public Opinion* (1973), is that, in a war with an uncertain purpose, a nation's public support for the war tends to fall as casualties among its troops rise.[8] This was true for both the Korean and Vietnam Wars, which looked to the U.S. public like bloody struggles for no clear, vital objectives. In the Korean War, U.S. military deaths rose early and fast (1950–1951) but then leveled off as stalemate set in (1952–1953). Conversely, public support for the Korean War fell early and fast, but then leveled off. In the Vietnam War, U.S. military deaths rose gradually but steadily over several years as the war incrementally escalated (1965–1968). Conversely, U.S. public support for the Vietnam War fell gradually but steadily over these same years. This trend of rising casualties and falling public support was *not* evident in World War II, a war with a clear and compelling purpose.

The key factor, then, is ambiguity of purpose. If the U.S. public has serious doubts about the value and clarity of the purpose of the war, its tolerance for casualties among its troops tends to be low. On the other hand, public tolerance for casualties among its troops tends to be high in a war for a clear and compelling purpose. During World War II, a war the U.S. public strongly believed had a clear and compelling purpose—remember Pearl Harbor!—we do not see the same casualty-sensitive dynamic in Mueller's poll numbers. U.S. public support for this "good" war remained high throughout World War II, even as U.S. casualties climbed.

Another crucial lesson of Vietnam that scholars, policy makers, and policy analysts learned was that public opinion is the "essential domino" in the process of taking the nation to war; if public opinion falls, other crucial dominoes in the U.S. political system—Congress, the national media, interest groups, political parties, and so on—begin falling as well. Leslie Gelb, director of the top-secret *Pentagon Papers* project for the Department of Defense, wrote in a 1972 *Foreign Affairs* article that "American public opinion was the essential domino" in the domestic political process; that is, U.S. public opinion was the "key stress point" in the U.S. political will to sustain the war in Vietnam.[9] Once public support for the war fell, the rest of the dominoes in the system would fall right behind. Because these other dominoes tend to tail after, rather than lead, public opinion, the loss of public support for the Vietnam War produced increased media criticism, increased congressional scrutiny, and increased critical opposition from antiwar groups and private interest groups (including some business groups and trade unions).[10]

These two critical factors—the centrality of public opinion and its connection to rising casualties in an ambiguous war— took on primary importance for political and military leaders in the decades following the Vietnam War. Together, these twin elements of the U.S. public's "Vietnam syndrome" (a pejorative term used by the Far Right) meant that U.S. leaders would either have to avoid embarking upon wars for which the purpose was ambiguous and U.S. casualties escalated or would invite the eventual (but inevitable) collapse of domestic political support, the humiliating withdrawal of U.S. troops, the loss of the war, and the destruction of the leaders' political and military careers. In other words, they would have to avoid dragging the United States into any new Vietnams.

THIRTY YEARS OF SUCCESS ... UNTIL 9/11

Over the three decades between the end of U.S. combat involvement in Vietnam and the beginning of the current war in Iraq, the above lessons proved successful in preventing the United States from again becoming bogged down in any new Vietnam-like quagmires. For example, in the early 1980s, war hawks and neocons in the Reagan administration wanted to commit U.S. ground combat troops to help the U.S.-backed government in El Salvador defeat a left-wing insurgency and to overthrow the leftist government in Nicaragua. However, fearing that a hawkish, ideologically driven "imperial presidency" might drag the United States into another Vietnam-style quagmire in Central America, Congress passed legislation to restrict the number of U.S. troops sent to El Salvador. Congress also passed the Boland Amendment to restrict military assistance to the right-wing "Contras," who were trying to overthrow the left-wing Sandinista government in Nicaragua. Additionally, the military chiefs argued vociferously against sending U.S. ground troops to Central America because there was no evidence that the U.S. public would support such a risky commitment, and intervening without public support risked bogging the United States down in a Vietnam-like quagmire in Central America.[11] The hawks and the neocons in the Reagan administration, facing such stiff resistance to direct U.S. combat involvement in Central America, then drove policy underground with covert and illegal alternatives such as the Iran-

Contra deal that caused such a scandal, once the deception was discovered and exposed by the international media.[12]

In June 1982, the neocons convinced President Reagan to give Israel a "green light" to invade Lebanon and wipe out the Palestine Liberation Organization (PLO), which was operating from southern Lebanon and conducting attacks on Israel. In their drive to Beirut in September 1982, the Israeli Defense Forces (IDF) surrounded two Palestinian refugee camps, Sabra and Shatila, and turned loose their ally, a Lebanese-Christian militia. The result was the massacre of between 700 and 800 Palestinian refugees, international condemnation of Israel, and the commitment of French, Italian, and U.S. "peacekeepers" (over Secretary of Defense Weinberger and the Joint Chiefs' strenuous objections) to a multisided, confusing civil war in Beirut.

In October 1983, with the Lebanese civil war no closer to ending and U.S. troops caught in the middle, a radical Lebanese-Muslim faction known as Hezbollah blew up the Marine barracks at Beirut's airport with a truck bomb, killing 239 Marines. Under intense pressure from Weinberger and the Joint Chiefs, Congress, the media, and public opinion, President Reagan soon withdrew the remaining 1,600 U.S. troops from Lebanon.

In the fall of the following year, President Ronald Reagan decided to end the Schultz-Weinberger feud over the use of force, and he endorsed the military's Vietnam-based conditions for the proper use of military force. Weinberger then made his now-famous speech proclaiming the military chiefs' six conditions for the proper use of force. Meanwhile, Secretary of State George Shultz and the neocons angrily charged that the military chiefs had become "wimps in uniform," suffering from a "Vietnam-Beirut syndrome."[13]

In the mid-to-late 1980s, the Weinberger Doctrine was successfully applied in the air raids against Libya (1986), the reflagging of Kuwaiti oil tankers in the Persian Gulf (1987), and the invasion of Panama (1989).[14] However, a much bigger test for the Weinberger Doctrine came with the first war against Iraq in 1991.

On August 2, 1990, Iraq invaded and occupied Kuwait, thereby waging an unprovoked, unnecessary, and illegal war. The United States responded by rushing rapid-reaction forces to Saudi Arabia to deter a possible Iraqi attack on Saudi oil fields. The United Nations Security Council, after careful discussion and debate, unanimously condemned Iraqi aggression against Kuwait and authorized the United States to lead a multinational coalition of military forces to reverse Iraqi aggression in Kuwait, degrade Iraq's conventional ability to invade its neighbors, and destroy Iraqi weapons of mass destruction (WMD) programs. The U.S. Congress also debated the wisdom of going to war against Iraq and in a very close vote, approved a war against Iraq to enforce the UN Resolution.[15]

As the U.S. generals and admirals with significant experience as younger officers in Vietnam contemplated war with Iraq, the potential for a disastrous quagmire was all too apparent to them.[16] Even Secretary of Defense Dick Cheney was keenly aware of how much the reputation of the post-Vietnam military was riding on Operation Desert Storm. Bob Woodward quoted Cheney in his book, *The Commanders,* as warning, "The military is finished in this society if we screw this up."[17]

However, General Colin Powell, chairman of the Joint Chiefs of Staff, made sure that the Weinberger Doctrine's conditions were met (he hated the label "the Powell Doctrine"), concluding that U.S. vital interests were at stake, political objectives were clear, sufficient force was applied, and domestic support was built. Indeed, according to Bob Woodward, it was Colin Powell who successfully pushed within Bush's inner circle for formal congressional authorization for the use of force before the war began, so that U.S. troops would not be left, yet again, "dangling out there" without domestic political support.[18]

The successful outcome of the first U.S. war against Iraq reaffirmed the Weinberger Doctrine and the military's lessons of Vietnam, despite President George Herbert Walker Bush's claim that the United States had finally "kicked the Vietnam syndrome."[19]

Post-Cold War tests of the lessons of Vietnam soon came with the mission to Somalia (Richard Holbrooke referred to it as the "Viet-malia syndrome"), the war in Bosnia, and the genocide in Rwanda. Colin Powell and the generals took much heat from an unexpected direction—the human rights and humanitarian assistance communities—for their opposition to using U.S. ground troops to nation-build in Somalia (1993) and stop "ethnic cleansing" genocide in Bosnia (1992–1995) and "machete" genocide in Rwanda (1994).[20] However, Presidents Bush (41) and Clinton must share primary responsibility for failing to understand the dangers of the *im*proper *non*use of force when it comes to halting humanity's worst crime.[21] Then came 9/11, and the neocons in the George W. Bush administration liquidated the lessons of Vietnam with the clever weapon of mass *deception.*

FIVE

❦

THE IRAQ QUAGMIRE

Woe to the statesman whose reasons for entering a war
do not appear so plausible at its end as at its beginning.
—*Otto von Bismarck*

The Iraq War the Bush administration launched in the spring of
2003 has become another Vietnam-like quagmire. It fits well the
pattern of massive, systematic fraud that presidential administrations from Truman through Nixon perpetrated against the U.S.
people in Vietnam. By late 2006, three and a half years later, the
United States was still mired in a "prolonged, bloody, ambiguous, and limited war" in Iraq.[1]

Bush's war in Iraq is "a war of choice, not necessity."[2] This
makes all the difference in the world, because wars of *choice*
are, and have been, *illegal* under international law for seventy-
five years, and *immoral* under the Western doctrine of Just War
for at least the past sixteen hundred years. According to Michael
Howard, the noted British scholar on war and strategy:

The Christian doctors, from Augustine to Aquinas in the Middle
Ages, followed by Francisco Suarez, Alberico Gentili, and Francisco

de Vitoria in the sixteenth century, were above all concerned with defining the just war, *jus ad bellum*: wars in which Christians might fight with a clear conscience. They laid down principles which still hold fairly good [*sic*] today. The war must be waged by a legitimate authority, for a cause itself just—to make reparation for an injury or to restore what had been wrongly seized—and in general with the intention of advancing good or avoiding evil.[3]

In positive international law, war has been prohibited, except for legitimate self-defense, by the Kellogg-Briand Pact of 1928, the UN Charter of 1945, and the Nuremberg Principles of 1946.[4]

The fact that the 2003 invasion of Iraq was a war of choice rather than necessity also makes all the difference in the world *strategically,* because an unsound purpose for a war inevitably produces unsuccessful strategy and tactics for fighting the war. You can reform the strategy and tactics all you want, but if you have an unsound purpose for the war, the best you can hope for is a better-executed failure, but it will still be a failure. Clausewitz pointed this out two hundred years ago, when he wrote: "The first, the supreme, the most far-reaching act of judgment that the statesman and the commander have to make is to establish by that test the kind of war on which they are embarked; neither mistaking it for, nor trying to turn it into, something alien to its nature. This is the first of all strategic questions and the most comprehensive."[5]

President George W. Bush and his advisers violated this first principle of war when they deceptively sold the nation an illegal and immoral war of *choice* by packaging it deceptively as a legal and moral war of *necessity.* Therefore, Bush's Iraq War policy has been dead in the water from day one. It cannot be salvaged; it must be scrapped. And every day, week, month, and year we delay doing so only adds to the final cost in precious lives (American and Iraqi) and tax dollars for a war that should never have been waged in the first place, and cannot possibly be won.

ENTERING: DECEPTION ABOUT PURPOSE

The initiation of the war in Iraq had nothing whatsoever to do with extremist Islamic terrorism. The Bush administration repeatedly implied that Saddam Hussein was behind the 9/11 attacks, that his regime had ties to al-Qaeda, and that Iraq possessed weapons of mass destruction (WMDs). These "facts" were strongly challenged by the U.S. intelligence community at the time, and they have been thoroughly discredited since then by the bipartisan 9/11 Commission and by the bipartisan Senate Select Committee on Intelligence.[6] Bush, Cheney, Rumsfeld, and the neocons either knew their "facts" were false or demonstrated "reckless disregard" for the truth as they steadily and deceptively marched the United States to war in Iraq. Their actions were malicious, and the consequences continue to be disastrous for Iraq, for the United States, and for the entire Middle East region.

For the architects of the Iraq War, 9/11 was simply a convenient excuse to wage a war they had long desired. The neocons yearned for years before 9/11 to invade and conquer Iraq as a prelude to "transforming" the entire Middle East into a solidly pro-U.S., pro-Israel region.[7] It had little or nothing to do with spreading "democracy" throughout the Middle East; that was just the idealistic packaging meant for domestic public consumption. The Bush administration's principal motive for waging war in Iraq in 2003 was to defend and extend American dominance in that critical region of the world. The best evidence for this is not to be found in books, articles, and speeches by Noam Chomsky and others on the Far Left, but in the writings of the most respected mainstream scholars and policy analysts, in the official governmental documents, and in the words of the neocons themselves. Indeed, the neocons are proud to be "imperialists," and in fact boast about it.

Neocon Robert Kaplan, in his recent book *Imperial Grunts: The American Military on the Ground,* defines imperialism as "the demand for absolute, undefiled security at home [which] leads one to conquer the world."[8] Kaplan goes on to explain, in rather majestic terms, what he sees as the larger historical context of contemporary U.S. imperialism:

> To be an American in the first decade of the twenty-first century was to be present at a grand and fleeting moment, a moment that even if it lasted for several more decades would constitute but a flicker among the long march of hegemons that had calmed broad swaths of the globe.... Some denied the very fact of American empire, claiming a contradiction between an imperial strategy and American democratic values. They forgot that Rome, Venice, and Britain were the most morally enlightened states of our ages.... Liberalism at home and a pragmatic, at times ruthless policy abroad have not been uncommon in the history of empires.[9]

Apparently, Kaplan's conception of "liberalism at home" includes warrantless wiretaps, government surveillance of critics, and the selective suspension of habeas corpus.

Kaplan goes on to paint a romanticized picture of U.S. imperialism, comparing U.S. soldiers to the nineteenth-century British troops fighting hostile tribes in distant lands for queen and country. For instance, he writes: "[T]he drama of exotic new landscapes has always been central to the imperial experience."[10] Kaplan admits that U.S. soldiers and Marines do not see *themselves* in such romantic, imperial terms, but they unconsciously perform necessary "imperial maintenance." To Robert Kaplan, U.S. soldiers are "cannon fodder" for the preservation and expansion of the American Empire.[11]

Max Boot, another prominent neocon writer, warned that Americans must be prepared to be as ruthless and as savage as earlier imperial powers—and suffer occasional military losses—if the United States is to maintain its imperial position at the pinnacle of world power. Boot wrote:

> Any nation bent on imperial policing will suffer a few setbacks. The British army, in the course of Queen Victoria's little wars, suffered

major defeats with thousands of casualties in the First Afghan War (1842) and the Zulu War (1879). This did not appreciably dampen British determination to defend and expand the empire; it made them hunger for vengeance. If Americans cannot adopt a similarly bloody-minded attitude, then they have no business undertaking imperial policing.[12]

Perhaps it did not occur to Max Boot that the American people never knowingly adopted a policy of "imperial policing," but were tricked into supporting it by Bush administration policy makers who cynically employed the language of idealism—"freedom"— and the images of terror—such as a nuclear mushroom cloud—in order to gain popular support for their imperial dreams.

The first attempt by the neocons to put into policy their grand strategy of U.S. imperial primacy was in 1992, during the George H. W. Bush administration (Bush 41). Neocons Paul Wolfowitz and Zalmay Khalilzad (the current U.S. ambassador to Iraq), at the behest of their boss, Secretary of Defense Dick Cheney, put forth a draft "Defense Planning Guide" that explicitly aimed to prevent the rise of any challengers—whether hostile or friendly—to U.S. global hegemony in any region of the world. This was the policy version of neocon theorist Charles Krauthammer's "Unipolar Moment," what he viewed as a golden opportunity for the "lone superpower" to ensure its number one position in the world, through superior, unilateral military force, for the next "American century."[13] The neocons' draft Defense Planning Guide, however, was leaked (perhaps by General Colin Powell?) to the *New York Times* and caused such political outrage among our Western allies (and Russia and China) and such political backlash at home that Bush 41 rejected it. The neocons subsequently withdrew from the battle to lick their wounds and bide their time.[14]

During the Clinton years, the out-of-power neocons continued with their plan for U.S. imperial dominance over the world. In 1997, neocon theorists Robert Kagan and William Kristol founded the *Project for the New American Century*

(www.newamericancentury.org) for the purpose of creating
strategic principles that will "shape a new century favorable to
American principles and interests."[15] This neocon strategic vision of bending the global order to serve primarily U.S. national
interests was to be promulgated through "a Reaganite policy of
military strength and moral clarity."[16]

For the neocons, international law such as the Geneva Conventions and international organizations such as the United
Nations were annoying multilateral "traps" to be avoided in the
unilateral U.S. drive to establish a permanent position of world
primacy. Using military force to remove Saddam Hussein was
the key to their neocon imperial strategy in the Middle East, and
formally signing on to this strategic vision were Dick Cheney,
Donald Rumsfeld, Paul Wolfowitz, Richard Perle, I. Lewis
"Scooter" Libby, Zalmay Khalilzad, Jeb Bush, Norman Podhoretz, Francis Fukuyama, William J. Bennett, Elliott Abrams, and
Dan Quayle.[17]

Another important objective of the neocons' strategic vision
was to reverse the verdict of Vietnam. As discussed previously,
the neocon movement was born in the 1970s as a reaction to the
United States' loss in Vietnam. The founding fathers of the neocon movement were Norman Podhoretz and Irving Kristol. The
neocons rejected the popular explanation that the U.S. defeat in
Vietnam was caused by our failure to understand the limits of
military force. Rather, they believed that the United States had
gone "wobbly" in Vietnam and lacked the courage to use superior military force to achieve decisive victory.[18] As such, they
were the cocreators, with the old Cold Warriors, of the Far Right
School on the lessons of Vietnam, mentioned in the previous
chapter. They believed in the unsentimental, ruthless use of superior U.S. military power to achieve U.S. interests in the world.
Consequently, the neocons especially hated the "timidity" of
the Weinberger-Powell Doctrine and the cautious approach to
the use of force of the Joint Chiefs of Staff (whom the neocons
referred to as "wimps in uniform").[19] The neocons fought hard
for two decades to undo the military's lessons of Vietnam, finally
succeeding only by the deceptive use of 9/11.[20]

It is, perhaps, more than a little ironic that none of the tough-talking neocon hawks ever served in Vietnam when they were of military age. Despite ardently supporting the war at the time, they all had something better to do. For example, Dick Cheney sought and received five successive draft deferments because, as he explained, "I had other priorities." Paul Wolfowitz also received multiple student deferments during the Vietnam War, and John Bolton (current U.S. ambassador to the UN), like George W. Bush, avoided going to Vietnam by joining the National Guard. In a moment of candor, Bolton explained: "I confess, I had no desire to die in a Southeast Asian rice paddy."[21] Of course, neither did those who willingly served in Vietnam. Nevertheless, those who served in Vietnam willingly at least demonstrated the courage of their convictions by risking the "ultimate sacrifice."

This bitter irony was not lost on veterans of Vietnam in senior positions in the military and in Congress in the run-up to the current war in Iraq. For example, U.S. Senator and Vietnam veteran Chuck Hagel, a Republican from Nebraska, asked neocon Richard Perle if he would be willing to be in the "first wave" of U.S. forces going into Baghdad. The term *chicken hawk,* coined by Vietnam veterans to describe war hawks who avoided personal sacrifice in war—"chicken then, hawk now"—began to appear more often in the debate over the war in Iraq. Retired Colonel Andrew Bacevich, a West Point graduate, Vietnam veteran, longtime conservative, and professor of international relations at Boston University, wrote of Vice President Dick Cheney: "He is the embodiment of the 'chicken hawk'—someone who having managed to miss the war of his youth is all too eager to send *others* to risk death or dismemberment."[22]

Once the neocons were back in power with the George W. Bush administration (Bush 43), they returned to promulgating their strategic plan to get rid of Saddam and consolidate U.S. regional and global primacy. They succeeded in embedding their strategic vision in the 2002 National Security Strategy of the United States of America. This seminal document called for reaffirming "the essential role of American military strength" in the world so that U.S. military power would remain "beyond challenge" and would "dissuade future military competition."[23]

Bush 43's initial reaction to 9/11 was appropriate and embraced by a bipartisan, united America and a supportive world community. Bush's decision to wage war against the Taliban in Afghanistan in order to apprehend or kill Osama bin Laden and other al-Qaeda members was also appropriate and also popular at home and abroad. However, the decision to invade Iraq seemed to almost half of Americans and most of the world to be a "bridge too far." The reasons given seemed to many to be bogus, and the evidence seemed flimsy. From the very beginning of the Bush administration's reaction to 9/11, the neocons around Bush pushed for war against Iraq. Richard Clarke, White House chief of counterterrorism under Clinton and Bush 43, wrote that on the very evening of 9/11 he could see that "Rumsfeld and Wolfowitz were going to try to take advantage of this national tragedy to promote their agenda about Iraq."[24] Bob Woodward observed that Rumsfeld and Wolfowitz argued for war against Iraq four days after 9/11 at an emergency meeting at Camp David. Deputy Secretary of Defense Paul Wolfowitz asserted that there was a "10 to 15% chance" that Saddam was behind the attacks on 9/11.[25]

Bush at first focused on Afghanistan, where al-Qaeda was hiding. However, he instructed Richard Clarke, his counterterrorism expert, to look for evidence of Saddam's complicity in 9/11. After an exhaustive search Clarke sent President Bush a memo saying that all intelligence agencies and the departments in the federal government concluded that there was no connection between Saddam's regime and the 9/11 attacks.[26] Nevertheless, Bush and the neocons decided soon afterward to go to war against Iraq, claiming that Saddam had connections to al-Qaeda and weapons of mass destruction, even if they had to use phony intelligence to pull it off.[27] John Prados, an analyst with the National Security Archives in Washington, juxtaposed declassified intelligence documents on Iraq's WMD program and alleged connections to al-Qaeda with several key White House and State Department speeches used to build public support for the war in Iraq, such as President Bush's January 2003 State of the Union address and Secretary of State Colin Powell's February 2003 speech to the United Nations Security Council. Prados characterized the factual gap between them as "a case study in government dishonesty" that was "systematic and carried out purposefully."[28] James Risen, longtime national security correspondent for the *New York Times,* wrote that all doubts and objections raised within the U.S. intelligence community about Saddam's WMD program and his alleged connections to al-Qaeda were "stifled" by "enormous pressure" from the White House, which steadfastly ignored any intelligence that contradicted what Richard Clarke called their "received wisdom."[29] Finally, there is the leaked "Downing Street Memo" of July 2002—eight months before the invasion of Iraq—that quoted the head of British intelligence, Sir Richard Dearlove, as reporting that "Bush wanted to remove Saddam, through military action, justified by the conjunction of terrorism and WMD. But the intelligence and facts were being fixed around policy."[30]

The evidence is thus overwhelming that the Bush administration cynically and maliciously engaged in a premeditated, calculated, systematic campaign of deception to wage an unnecessary war against Iraq, which then backfired on them and mired the United States in a bloody, expensive quagmire in Iraq. As John Prados wrote in 2004: "The American people, subjected to a systematic effort to mislead, to frighten them into acquiescence, lost a measure of the checks and balances that hold back the dogs of war, and are still paying the price in blood and treasure for Bush's folly. We have been suckered into a Middle East maelstrom from which extrication may prove exceedingly difficult."[31]

Richard Clarke, a nonpartisan intelligence professional who served both Democratic and Republican presidents faithfully for many years, wrote bitterly:

It is not hard to understand why, after repeatedly hearing remarks [about how the War on Terrorism began on 9/11] that 70 percent of the American people believed that Saddam Hussein had attacked the

Pentagon and the World Trade Center. I suspect that many heroic U.S. troops who risked their lives fighting in Iraq thought, because of misleading statements from the White House, that they were avenging the 3,000 dead from September 11. What a horrible thing it was to give such a false impression to our people and our troops.[32]

It was, indeed, a "horrible thing," a dirty deed that only got worse as the Bush administration engaged in additional deception to sink the nation deeper into the Iraq quagmire.

SINKING DEEPER: DECEPTION ABOUT PROGRESS

After the initial victorious march to Baghdad in the spring of 2003, the Bush administration tried to convince the U.S. public that continued Iraqi resistance was just the last throes of a defeated regime, "dead-enders" putting up a useless, last-ditch fight. However, it soon became apparent to the rest of the world that a serious and lethal anti-occupation insurgency had begun. The first major public figure to draw the Vietnam analogy two months into the war was Army Chief of Staff General Eric Shinsecki.[33] Suddenly, U.S. troops found themselves having to relearn counterinsurgency lessons about "winning hearts and minds" first learned more than thirty years earlier in Vietnam. Bush, Cheney, Rumsfeld, and others in the administration deceptively used the term *terrorists* to describe to the American people those fighters violently resisting U.S. occupation. For example, in the summer of 2003, Secretary of Defense Donald Rumsfeld said, "I guess the reason I don't use the phrase 'guerrilla war' is because there isn't one." However, only a few weeks later General John Abizaid, commander of U.S. forces in the Middle East, said that the U.S. military was facing a "classical guerrilla-style campaign" in Iraq.[34] The Bush administration was well aware that intelligence indicated that somewhere between 90 percent and 96 percent of the insurgents in Iraq were homegrown nationalists, and that only a relatively small number were foreign fighters with ties to radical terrorist groups.[35]

The U.S.-created and -supported Iraqi government has been largely incompetent and corrupt, and the Iraqi military has had little incentive to fight so long as U.S. troops remain there to do the job for them.[36] According to David Phillips, who served in Iraq as a senior adviser on nation-building with the U.S. State Department, sincere efforts at nation-building in Iraq were ruined by the neocon ideologues in the Bush administration, who seemed more committed to transforming the Middle East into a U.S.-dominated region than to helping the Iraqi people.[37] (This was also true three decades ago in Vietnam.) According to Larry Diamond, senior adviser for democratic development with the Coalition Provisional Authority (CPA) in Iraq, U.S. Ambassador Paul Bremer, appointed by Bush to head the CPA, actually blocked plans for democratic municipal Iraqi elections so that the United States could remain in overall control of Iraqi political developments.[38]

Meanwhile, the Bush administration regularly assured the American public that real progress was being made in defeating the insurgents and in "nation-building" in Iraq, especially from 2006–2007 as the war dragged on, U.S. casualties steadily climbed, and public support for the war declined. For instance, in the spring of 2005, Vice President Dick Cheney stated: "The level of activity that we see today, from a military standpoint, I think will clearly decline. I think they're in the last throes, if you will, of the insurgency."[39] In the summer of 2005, President George W. Bush said: "These terrorists and insurgents ... will fail.... We have a strategy for success in Iraq.... As Iraqis stand up, Americans and coalition forces will stand down. And we're making progress. More and more Iraqi units are more and more capable of defending themselves."[40] And in the fall of 2005, Secretary of State Condoleezza Rice said, "Time and time again, people are coming now to support for Iraq.... We have made significant progress."[41]

However, this public relations campaign of official optimism was belied by the facts on the ground. In truth, the Iraqi insurgency was getting much stronger, and the "nation-building" program was paralyzed. For the first twenty months of the insurgency, the U.S. military, under Rumsfeld and Bremer's direction, used conventional war fighting tactics against an unconventional enemy (just as the United States had thirty years earlier in Vietnam). The U.S. military kept launching large-scale operations against insurgency strongholds such as Fallujah, Ramadi, Samara, and Mosul, taking and retaking those cities in 2003, 2004, 2005, and 2006.[42] The U.S. military was trying to apply its strategy of "clear, hold, and build." But the insurgents, who were able to replace their losses fairly easily, responded with their own strategy of "recoil, redeploy, and spoil." The use of excessive (conventional) force, along with mass roundups, detention, and torture, has decreased the legitimacy of the U.S. and coalition forces and increased the legitimacy of the insurgency in the eyes of many Iraqis.[43]

At this point, the United States is facing not one but two robust and growing insurgencies in Iraq: a nationalist Sunni insurgency and a radical Shiite insurgency. These two insurgencies are also waging a low-level civil war against each other. Meanwhile, the Sunni Kurds are trying to protect their lucrative oil holdings in northern Iraq. The much-respected national security analyst, Anthony Cordesman, recently wrote that every indicator now shows that the United States is losing the war in Iraq.[44] Two senior U.S. generals told the Senate Armed Services Committee in late summer 2006 that Iraqi sectarian violence was worsening and could lead to open civil war and the partition of Iraq. General John Abizaid, commander of U.S. forces in the region, and General Peter Pace, chairman of the Joint Chiefs of Staff, told the Senate committee that the situation in Iraq was the worst since the war started three and a half years earlier. Neither general could tell the committee when the insurgents would be defeated, when the Iraqi army would be capable of standing on its own, or when U.S. troops could begin coming home.[45] On September 19, 2006, General Abizaid said that more than 140,000 U.S. troops—and maybe more—would probably be needed in Iraq until at least spring 2007 because of how bad the security situation in Iraq had become. He acknowledged that finding more U.S. troops to send to Iraq would be a challenge.[46]

HITTING BOTTOM: DECEPTION ABOUT METHODS

The Bush administration deceived the U.S. public about the methods the United States is using to fight the war in Iraq, such as torturing detainees and intentionally killing unarmed Iraqi civilians. Administration officials have tried to convince the U.S. public that the discovered incidents of torture and murder are "isolated incidents" perpetrated by "a few bad apples" in the lowest ranks of the military. However, the multiplicity of incidents and the mounting facts surrounding them paint a far different picture, one of a larger pattern of intentional, systematic misuse of force intended to terrorize the Iraqi population into breaking with the insurgency. Because this strategy has backfired and made the insurgency stronger, and because U.S. troops are now caught in the middle of a nasty civil war, the morale of U.S. troops in Iraq has begun to decline precipitously. When one adds to this the steady decline of public and congressional support for the Iraq War back home, it becomes clear (just as it did thirty years ago in Vietnam) that continuing the war in Iraq is useless.

On April 30, 2004, *The New Yorker* magazine posted on its Web site Seymour Hersh's story about U.S. torture and sexual abuse of Iraqi prisoners at Abu Ghraib prison, thirty miles west of Baghdad. Explicit, horrifying graphic pictures of the torture were included.[47] Ironically, Hersh was the journalist who uncovered the My Lai massacre in Vietnam more than three decades earlier. The Abu Ghraib torture story triggered a firestorm of international and domestic criticism of U.S. behavior in Iraq. Apparently, someone had leaked to Seymour Hersh a secret

U.S. Army report of an investigation of the Abu Ghraib torture allegations, complete with color photos and video. The report, written by Major General Antonio Taguba, concluded, "several U.S. Army soldiers have committed egregious acts and grave breaches of international law at Abu Ghraib . . . and Camp Bucca, Iraq."[48] General Taguba pointed out in the report that the abuses under investigation at these two U.S.-run prisons occurred in the wake of Major General Geoffrey Miller's visit to Iraq to instruct the U.S. guard force "in setting the conditions" of interrogation techniques already in use at Guantánamo Prison in Cuba.[49] Although the Bush administration claimed that the abuses at Abu Ghraib were carried out by just a "few bad apples" in the Army, Hersh's investigation showed that U.S. torture was systematically applied in Iraq, in Afghanistan, in Cuba, and in secret U.S. interrogation centers around the world. Hersh uncovered a top-secret program, authorized by President Bush on September 7, 2002, and code named "Copper Green" (the color of field telephone electrodes?) to apply to terrorists captured anywhere in the world—torture techniques that violated the Geneva Conventions of 1949, the UN Convention Against Torture ratified by the United States in 1994, and U.S. federal law. Secretary of Defense Donald Rumsfeld implemented the program, and Vice President Dick Cheney covered it up.[50]

Allegations of U.S. torture and prisoner abuse were not a surprise to the International Committee of the Red Cross (ICRC), official protector of prisoner-of-war rights since the middle of the nineteenth century. The ICRC had been quietly complaining for some time to the Coalition Forces about U.S. treatment of Iraqi prisoners being held at Abu Ghraib and elsewhere, but Rumsfeld's Pentagon turned a deaf ear to them.[51] The executive director of Human Rights Watch, the most respected human rights organization in the world, sent a letter of protest to President Bush stating:

> U.S. forces have systematically mistreated detainees in Iraq, Afghanistan, Guantánamo, and elsewhere. These violations of international

law governing the treatment of detainees threaten to erode human rights norms that protect everyone taken into custody, including Americans. They have also done enormous damage to America's reputation, harmed U.S. efforts to build global support for countering terrorism, and been an apparent boon to terrorist recruiters.[52]

Professor Andrew Bacevich of Boston University, a graduate of West Point, labeled Abu Ghraib "the greatest shame to befall the Army since Vietnam itself."[53]

Added to the torture scandal is the rash of criminal cases being brought against U.S. Army soldiers and Marines for illegally killing unarmed Iraqi civilians. The worst cases involved Marines who were accused of slaughtering twenty-four Iraqi men, women, and children in several households in Haditha on November 19, 2005, in retaliation for a roadside bomb that killed one Marine in their squad, and U.S. soldiers who were accused of raping a young Iraqi girl and then killing her and her entire family in Mahmudiya on March 12, 2006. Some U.S. military analysts suggested that the new crop of war crime cases is the result of an increasingly ambiguous war with no end in sight.[54] Others suggest that U.S. atrocities against Iraqi civilians, as well as the torture of Iraqi prisoners, are indicative of U.S. troops dehumanizing their enemy in Iraq, just as they had in Vietnam three decades earlier.[55] However, we must remember that the Bush administration's intentional deception created the Iraq quagmire and its strategically ambiguous environment in which U.S. troops are confused about who their enemy is, when to use lethal force, and why they are still fighting in Iraq.[56] According to leading international law scholars in the United States—from the American Bar Association, the Center for Constitutional Rights, the American Civil Liberties Union, and Human Rights First—it is to the most senior levels of political and military leadership in the Bush administration that we must look for "command responsibility" for war crimes in Iraq.[57] Perhaps the words of U.S. Supreme Court Justice Robert Jackson, chief U.S. prosecutor at the 1946 Nuremberg Trial, bear repeating here:

"We must never forget that the record on which we judge these defendants today is the record on which history will judge us tomorrow."[58]

BLOCKING THE EXIT: DECEPTION ABOUT THE DIFFICULTY OF WITHDRAWAL

In early fall 2006, the Bush administration, faced with a disastrous war policy in Iraq, chose to wage a last-ditch effort to convince the U.S. public that real progress is being made, that withdrawing from Iraq immediately would increase the terrorist threat to the United States, and that if the American people would just remain patient a little bit longer, light would soon appear at the end of the Iraq tunnel. At the same time, the administration's chicken hawks were viciously "swift-boating" their critics, using the usual surrogates to malign honest, courageous, highly decorated Americans, such as John Kerry, Max Cleland, and John Murtha, calling them "cut-and-run cowards."[59] With real hope of U.S. "victory" in Iraq disappearing, the Bush administration's ultimate aim seemed to be to hold out long enough to pass the Iraq mess off to the next president, just as Lyndon Johnson did with Vietnam.[60] To accomplish this, the Bush administration seemed prepared to do whatever was necessary—including violating the U.S. Constitution—to keep its critics from forcing the administration to take responsibility for a failed war ... just as Richard Nixon did during Vietnam. But with the Republican Party's devastating loss of both houses of Congress in the November election and the increasing political isolation of the White House, Bush was forced to change his strategy again, this time to one of (apparent) flexibility on a solution to the war in Iraq. At this writing, in late November 2006, Bush's sincerity regarding his newfound flexibility has yet to be demonstrated.

SIX

꩜

Last Exit from Baghdad

Cut and run? You bet.
—*Lt. Gen. William E. Odom*

U.S. political and military leaders created the Iraq quagmire using systematic deception for both ideological motives and personal political gain. In this centrally strategic way, Iraq is Vietnam's identical twin, separated by thirty years of neocon labor. And because the United States did not fully grasp the appropriate lessons of Vietnam, the Iraq quagmire seems headed for the same tragic outcome as the Vietnam quagmire: disastrous defeat and humiliating withdrawal.

So where does this leave us? Unfortunately, it leaves us with an exhausted, increasingly dispirited Army wanting out of Iraq; a disillusioned, skeptical public wanting its troops home; an increasingly desperate Bush administration hoping to snatch victory from the jaws of defeat; an increasingly hopeful Democratic Party trying to forge an alternative solution that will win it the White House; a weak, somewhat unimaginative antiwar movement trying to re-create the 1960s, and the real potential

89

for at least two more years of bloody stalemate in Iraq. There is a chance, however, of exiting the Iraq quagmire sooner.

BROKEN ARMY

The Army in Iraq is an overstretched, frustrated force that seems to be playing "Whack a Mole," according to Senator John McCain.[1] Every time U.S. forces flood a troubled area of Iraq—Fallujah, Ramadi, or Baghdad—the insurgents disappear only to pop up somewhere else. Because U.S. commanders do not have enough forces to flood all of the cities and towns in Iraq, the insurgents can play this game indefinitely. Meanwhile, U.S. troops on their second or third tour in Iraq see a worsening situation, rather than the "progress" that Washington has been perpetually heralding.

There are really no active-duty Army brigades that can be sent to reinforce U.S. troops in Iraq for more than a brief period. According to Pentagon analyst Larry Korb, who served as assistant secretary of defense in the Reagan administration, one-third of all Army brigades are in Iraq or Afghanistan, and almost two-thirds are in the process of recovering, retraining, and refitting from their last tour in Iraq or Afghanistan. The few brigades not in this "unready" state are stationed in Japan and South Korea and can be sent to Iraq only by abandoning U.S. security interests in Asia. The Army Reserve and National Guard will be of little help in this crisis, because they are in even worse shape than the active Army brigades, having left all of their equipment—the tanks, trucks, and Humvees—in Iraq when they left to come home. This dire manpower and equipment shortage in the Army (and replicated in the Marines) had been confirmed by two earlier independent reports, one by retired Colonel Andrew Krepinevich, under contract for the Pentagon, and the second by the Rand Corporation. The chief source of this stress on the Army's personnel and equipment is the unanticipated length of the war in Iraq.[2]

Some political leaders have called for expanding the overall size of the Army as a solution to the current severe manpower shortages, but the reality is that the Army has already had to lower its enlistment standards considerably to attract enough recruits to address existing manpower needs, accepting high school dropouts, applicants with criminal records, and the intellectually challenged. Even with these lower standards, Army recruiters have had to bend the rules to meet their quotas because "no one wants to join."[3] Lowering the recruitment standards still further is no solution, either, as it would almost certainly take the Army back to the bottom-of-the-barrel, bad old days of the Vietnam era. Retention of experienced, skilled combat soldiers is also getting tougher for the Army. Consequently, the Army has resorted to "stop loss" procedures to keep soldiers beyond the end of their enlistment contracts, which has created serious morale problems among the troops.[4] The only alternative left, then, for increasing the size of the Army is to bring back the draft, which Congress views (accurately) as "political suicide" and therefore beyond rational consideration. In light of these hard, ugly realities, the burning question now for those with close ties to the Army's top generals is: How much longer can the Iraq War continue before the U.S. Army (and Marine Corps) breaks down completely, the way it did in Vietnam in 1970–1971?[5] Very soon, now (to paraphrase Larry Korb), the Army that was sent to Iraq to save the Iraqi people will have to withdraw to save itself.

THE "ESSENTIAL DOMINO" FALLS

Public opinion in the United States on the war in Iraq has declined so far that an overwhelming majority of Americans now believe that invading Iraq was a mistake. As political analyst Dick Polman wrote: "2005 might well be remembered as the year when public opinion went south and never came back—a mood shift roughly analogous to 1968, when domestic confidence in the Vietnam War began its irreversible slide."[6]

According to a CNN/USA Today/Gallup poll, in March 2003, only 23 percent of Americans thought invading Iraq was a "mistake." By October 2004, that number had more than doubled to 47 percent, and in February 2006, the percentage of Americans concluding the war was a mistake had risen to 55 percent.[7] John Mueller, professor of political science at Ohio State University and the author in 1973 of a groundbreaking work on the relationship between rising troop casualties and falling public support for a war, recently wrote in *Foreign Affairs*:

> American troops have been sent into harm's way many times since 1945, but in only three cases—Korea, Vietnam, and Iraq—have they been drawn into sustained ground combat and suffered more than 300 deaths in action. American public opinion became a key factor in all three wars, and in each one there has been a simple association: as casualties mount, support decreases. Broad enthusiasm at the outset invariably erodes. The only thing remarkable about the current war in Iraq is how precipitously American support has dropped off. Casualty for casualty, support has declined far more quickly than it did during either the Korean War or the Vietnam War. And if history is any indication, there is little the Bush administration can do to reverse this decline.[8]

And a *New York Times* article on public opinion and the Iraq War published in July 2006 observed that "no military conflict in modern times has divided Americans on partisan lines more than the war in Iraq, scholars and pollsters say—not even Vietnam."[9]

The U.S. public is deeply concerned about rising U.S. casualties in Iraq and no longer believes that the Iraq War has anything to do with the larger war on terrorism. The public seems restless about current policy in Iraq, impatient to see U.S. troops come home, and increasingly angry with elected officials for failing to win the war and for deceiving them about the purpose of the war in the first place. And it is highly unlikely that, no matter what the Bush administration says or does, the U.S. public can be won back to supporting the war.

Congress, "that sapless branch," has a propensity to follow public opinion rather than lead it. As public opinion goes, so goes Congress. Therefore, Congress has separated itself from the administration's war in Iraq. The 2006 midterm election provided clear, unequivocal evidence of this political shift. The election outcome, driven primarily by national anxiety over the war in Iraq, gave both houses of Congress to the president's opposition, the Democratic Party. Within days of the election, Bush asked for Secretary of Defense Donald Rumsfeld's resignation and nominated as his replacement Robert Gates, a much more moderate Republican from his father's administration.

The Democratic Party's leadership certainly has benefited from the dramatic shift in the direction of the political "wind" in the United States, but it has not yet adopted an official position on what to do about the quagmire in Iraq, with John Kerry, John Murtha, Russ Feingold, and Nancy Pelosi pressing for a timetable for U.S. withdrawal and Hillary Clinton and Mark Warner opposing a definitive exit date. Consequently, most Americans have little faith at this time in a Democratic Party solution to the Iraq debacle.[10]

The antiwar movement, to the extent that it exists, often seems old and unimaginative in its strategies, tactics, and rhetoric. It is as though its leaders, having gained an incomplete understanding of the lessons from Vietnam (e.g., the military's), and a limited strategic sense about political change over the last thirty years, too often appear to be trying to re-create the antiwar movement of the 1960s. Hence, the Iraq antiwar movement has, so far, remained relatively small and marginally effective. Surely, the absence of a military draft contributes to this situation, but it cannot explain it completely. However, this may change quickly if political elites in both parties fail to force the Bush administration to withdraw U.S. troops from Iraq in the next six to twelve months. The rapidly growing political opposition to the Iraq War may soon be forced into the streets, which will not be the best alternative to staying in Iraq. The recent election clearly signaled that the patience of the U.S. electorate has run out on Iraq, and the ability of the U.S. military to sustain the war in Iraq—without "breaking" the institution—is exhausted.[11] Combined, these two hard, bitter political facts of life now define the parameters of strategic reality for all future "solutions" to the Iraq quagmire. *Any proposed "exit plan" that fails to take this strategic reality into account, regardless of who proposes it, will be "dead on arrival."*

ANY SOLUTION?

The present predicament indicates the real possibility of at least two more years of bloody stalemate in Iraq, coupled with increasing political chaos at home. The Bush administration will probably not end the U.S. war in Iraq, and Congress, on its own, lacks the institutional backbone to force the president to withdraw from Iraq anytime soon. The Iraq Study Group (www. usip.isg), created by Congress with the reluctant blessing of the Bush White House, came forth with its recommendations for a change in U.S. strategy in Iraq. However, this body of experts has carefully excluded from its deliberations all of the authoritative voices calling for a rapid withdrawal of U.S. troops from Iraq, such as Congressmember John Murtha and General William Odom. Therefore, the Iraq Study Group is unlikely to recommend the rapid withdrawal of U.S. forces from Iraq.

So the American people may have to wait at least until the next administration takes office in early 2009 to witness the withdrawal of all U.S. troops from Iraq. Even then, it will take a far more enlightened and united Democratic Party leadership than we have now to bring U.S. troops home in a timely and well-considered manner.

So is there no alternative to protracted, bloody stalemate in Iraq? Theoretically, there is a chance to build an unusual U.S. political coalition that will present a clear strategy for a rapid and responsible U.S. troop withdrawal from Iraq. This strategy would also convince legitimate international and regional organizations to broker a comprehensive compromise among Iraqi factions and between Iraq and its neighbors that would permit the violence in Iraq to subside, stability to emerge, and economic, political, and social development to resume. Such an innovative political coalition would necessitate some strange political bedfellows in U.S. politics. It would require Democratic-Republican bipartisanship, liberal-conservative cooperation, and government-corporate-academic sector collaboration. Constructing such an effective opposition to the current dead-end policy in Iraq will, however, require extraordinary political maturity, flexibility, and vision. These requirements then rule out the participation of the Far Left and the Far Right, but that is a good thing. In essence, it would require rebuilding the unusual coalition that existed in the United States—and that had many, many friends around the world—in the days and weeks after September 11, 2001. To turn such a theoretical opportunity into a practical reality, we must begin by identifying a core group of leading individuals from these disparate U.S. communities who have demonstrated strategic vision, political flexibility, and personal courage on the problem of the Iraq War.

THE "WISE MEN AND WOMEN"

This core might include former National Security Agency director General William Odom, Republican Senator Chuck Hagel, Democratic Representative John Murtha, counterterrorist expert Richard Clarke, former national security advisers Zbigniew Brzezinski and General Brent Scowcroft, former Middle East regional commander General Anthony Zinni, former NATO commander General Wesley Clark, former secretaries of state Madeleine Albright and Colin Powell, 9/11 Commission chair Tom Kean and vice chair Lee Hamilton, former Supreme Court Justice Sandra Day O'Connor, international relations professors John Mearsheimer, John Mueller, and Stephen Walt, and journalists Seymour Hersh and Thomas Ricks. (As mentioned previously, the Iraq Study Group's "wise men and women" excluded from its membership expert voices recommending rapid withdrawal, such as Odom and Murtha. They also failed to include journalists with considerable expertise on the Iraq War, such as Seymour Hersh and Thomas Ricks.)

First and foremost in an "exit strategy" must be the rapid withdrawal of U.S. military forces from Iraq. As General Odom argued recently in the pages of *Foreign Policy:*

> Only with rapid withdrawal from Iraq will Washington regain diplomatic and military mobility. Tied down like Gulliver in the sands of Mesopotamia, we simply cannot attract the diplomatic and military cooperation necessary to win the real battle against terror. Getting out of Iraq is the precondition for any improvement. In fact, getting out now may be our only chance to set things right in Iraq.[12]

Several other policy experts have echoed this important point. Larry Diamond of the Hoover Institution at Stanford wrote that the more nationalist-minded insurgents, the bulk of the Iraqi resistance, might well scale back their insurgency if the UN, the EU, and the Arab League could persuade the United States to remove its troops from Iraq.[13] Leslie Gelb, president emeritus of the prestigious Council on Foreign Relations, insisted that the United States must work with the UN, the EU, and regional states (such as Saudi Arabia, Syria, and Iran) to find a diplomatic solution that keeps a decentralized Iraq united and peaceful.[14] A European foreign minister told Seymour Hersh that "an international conference is important to stabilize the [Iraq] situation," but that the Bush administration will not negotiate with Iraq's neighbors, and the Europeans will not become deeply involved until the U.S. government changes its strategy in Iraq.[15] In the wake of the 2006 election, the Bush administration's policy of refusing to talk with Syria and Iran about bringing stability in Iraq may be changing. If so, that would be a hopeful sign. Persuading Syria and Iran to pressure their clients, the Sunni insurgents and the Shiite militias, to cease their bloody feuding and negotiate their differences through the political process would greatly ease a U.S. military withdrawal. The bottom line, however, is that U.S. troop withdrawals cannot be contingent upon progress on the diplomatic front; U.S. troops must come home soon, regardless of the diplomatic situation.

Some Americans might wonder if a rapid troop withdrawal, followed by international diplomacy, would squander the sacrifice of U.S. troops in Iraq and undermine their morale. However, General Odom explained that most troops want to come home sooner rather than later, and the results of a recent Zogby poll of U.S. troops in Iraq confirm this fact.[16] Some Americans might wonder if withdrawing U.S. troops before the insurgency is defeated will, as President Bush has repeatedly asserted, make the global terrorist threat against the United States worse. However, an April 2006 National Intelligence Estimate, representing the consensus view of all sixteen intelligence organizations that make up the U.S. intelligence community, found that the U.S. war in Iraq has actually *worsened* the threat of radical Islamic terrorism, as critics of the war had predicted even before the war began in March 2003.[17] Some Americans might wonder if pulling out of Iraq "before the job is done" will irreparably damage U.S. credibility in the world. However, Zbigniew Brzezinski has pointed out that the U.S. war in Iraq has already

> gravely undermined American global credibility. It has even more seriously compromised us morally. It has shown the limits of our warfare capability for dealing with political conflicts. It has cost tens of billions of dollars more than originally estimated. And it would take a very naïve president to again succumb to the same people who first demagogued about the need to go to war, who vastly exaggerated the welcome we would receive, who mismanaged the political dimensions of the war.[18]

THE LESSONS OF IRAQ

The opposition to the war in Iraq will succeed in ending that war someday, and U.S. troops will finally come home. But the effort cannot end there. We must be sure to reinforce the lessons learned in Vietnam and reaffirmed in Iraq, lessons that were identified by the three mainstream schools on the lessons of Vietnam: the Conservative, Liberal, and Military Schools. The first lesson to relearn is the limitations of military force. Carl von Clausewitz wrote that *purpose* is the single most important element in the politico-military process of taking a nation to war.[19] But if the political purpose of a war contradicts the nation's fundamental values, the nation will not long sustain it. It is a *foolish* mistake to fail to match political purpose to vital national interests and values. However, it is a *malicious* mistake to wage such a war by deceiving, intentionally and in a premeditated fashion, the people who must pay the bills for the war in blood and treasure. The noted historian Martin van Creveld, professor of military history at Hebrew University, addressed this crucial point recently: "For misleading the American people, and launching the most foolish war since Emperor Augustus in 9 B.C. sent his legions into Germany and lost them, Bush deserves to be impeached and, once he has been removed from office, put on trial along with the rest of the president's men. If convicted, they'll have plenty of time to mull over their sins."[20]

The second lesson to be relearned is the continuing relevance of international law, especially the laws of war. A nation that loses sight of this will forfeit the moral high ground in international relations and make itself the world's pariah. The third lesson to reaffirm is the importance of preserving U.S. constitutional law, for it makes little sense to preach democracy internationally while allowing the "imperial presidency" to undermine constitutional rights domestically. The fourth lesson is the importance of multilateralism in foreign policy. No nation, regardless of how strong it might be militarily and economically, can police the world by itself. Today's global problems—and global opportunities—are too many and too complex for any nation to manage alone; these global challenges require cooperative international leadership rather than imperial unilateralism. As we have seen with both the Vietnam and Iraq quagmires—and as the former Soviet Union also learned in Afghanistan—popularly supported insurgents can tie down and exhaust the greatest "superpowers," particularly if they lack support from the larger international community. As Loch Johnson, professor of public and international affairs at the University of Georgia, wrote recently: "The United States can exercise only a limited influence over the affairs of other nations. America's experience in Indochina should have seared that lesson into the nation's memory.... Now, History—the sternest of taskmasters—is repeating the lesson in Iraq."[21] Only by relearning and reteaching these crucial lessons can we help our children and their children avoid bloody quagmires in the future.

Notes

NOTES FOR PREFACE

1. Thomas Ricks, *Fiasco: The American Military Adventure in Iraq* (New York: Penguin Press, 2006).

NOTES FOR CHAPTER 1

1. Jeffrey Record and W. Andrew Terrill, *Iraq and Vietnam: Differences, Similarities, and Insights* (Carlisle Barracks, PA: U.S. Army War College, 2004), vii.

2. Ibid.

3. Ibid., 51.

4. Ibid., 7.

5. Christopher Hitchens, "Beating a Dead Parrot: Why Iraq and Vietnam Have Nothing Whatsoever in Common," *Slate* (January 31, 2005), slate.msn.com (accessed February 22, 2005).

6. Ibid.

7. Melvin Laird, "Iraq: Learning the Lessons of Vietnam," *Foreign Affairs* 84 (November/December 2005), www.foreignaffairs.org (accessed October 19, 2005).

8. Ibid.

9. Ibid.

10. Stephen Biddle, "Seeing Baghdad, Thinking Saigon," *Foreign Affairs* 86 (March/April 2006), www.foreignaffairs.org (accessed March 1, 2006).

11. Daniel Ellsberg, "The Courage to Talk Withdrawal" (June 9, 2005), www.antiwar.com (accessed June 18, 2005).

12. Lawrence Freedman, "The Iraq Syndrome: Like McNamara in Vietnam, Rumsfeld Will Leave a Legacy," *Washington Post National Weekly Edition* (January 17-23, 2005): 22-23.

13. "Hagel: Iraq Growing More Like Vietnam," *CNN* (August 18, 2005), www.cnn.com (accessed August 20, 2005).

14. John E. Mueller, *War, Presidents, and Public Opinion* (New York: John Wiley and Sons, 1973).

15. John E. Mueller, "The Iraq Syndrome," *Foreign Affairs* 84 (November/December 2005): 44-54.

16. Martin van Creveld, "Costly Withdrawal Is the Price to Be Paid for a Foolish War," *Forward* (November 25, 2005), www.forward.com (accessed January 25, 2006).

17. William E. Odom, "Iraq Through the Prism of Vietnam," *Neiman Watchdog* (March 8, 2006), www.truthout.org (accessed March 12, 2006).

18. *The American Heritage Dictionary of the English Language,* s.v. "Quagmire."

19. Lawrence Freedman, "Escalators and Quagmires: Expectations and the Use of Force," *International Affairs* 67:1 (1991): 26; David Halberstam, *The Making of a Quagmire* (New York: Random House, 1964).

20. British historian Sir Martin Gilbert reflects this view of war in his book *The First World War: A Complete History* (New York: Henry Holt, 2004).

21. See Winston S. Churchill, *The Second World War,* Volume One: *The Gathering Storm* (New York: Houghton Mifflin, 1948), and Raul Hilberg, *The Destruction of the European Jews* (Chicago: Quadrangle Books, 1961).

22. See W. Michael Reisman and Chris T. Antoniou, eds., *The Laws of War: A Comprehensive Collection of Primary Documents on International Law Governing Armed Conflict* (New York: Vintage Books, 1994); Michael R. Marrus, *The Nuremberg War Crimes Trial 1945-46: A Documentary History* (Boston: Bedford Books, 1997); and William Schabas, *Genocide in International Law* (Cambridge: Cambridge University Press, 2000).

NOTES FOR CHAPTER 2

1. Philip Caputo, *A Rumor of War* (New York: Owl Books, 1977/1996), 36.

2. The "rabbit lesson" was described quite accurately by former Marine Sergeant Joe Bangert at the "Winter Soldier Investigation" in Detroit in January 1971. See the documentary film *Winter Soldier* (Winterfilm/Millennium, 1972/2005).

NOTES FOR CHAPTER 3

1. John J. Mearsheimer, *The Tragedy of Great Power Politics* (New York: Norton, 2001), 25.

2. Chair of the Joint Chiefs of Staff Lyman Lemnitzer, quoted in James S. Olson and Randy Roberts, *Where the Domino Fell: America and Vietnam 1945-2004*, 4th ed. (Maplecrest, NY: Brandywine Press, 2004), 82.

3. This was a phrase commonly heard in Vietnam and apparently is echoing these days in Iraq. Its derivation is the early thirteenth-century crusade against the Albigensian heretics in southern France. The papal legate Arnaud, when asked by the commander of the crusaders how they were to recognize the heretics from true believers in the Albigensian town of Languedoc, replied, "Kill them all, for God knows His own." The crusaders then massacred the town's entire population of men, women, and children. See Will Durant, *The Story of Civilization,* Volume IV: *The Age of Faith* (New York: Simon and Schuster, 1950), 774-775.

4. George McTurnan Kahin, *Intervention: How America Became Involved in Vietnam* (Garden City, NJ: Anchor, 1987), 7-8.

5. Ellen J. Hammer, *The Struggle for Indochina, 1940-1955* (Stanford, CA: Stanford University Press, 1955), 325.

6. Kahin, *Intervention*, 35.

7. Ibid., 45-48.

8. U.S. Central Intelligence Agency, *Special National Intelligence Estimate SNIE 10-4-54* (Top Secret), "Communist Reactions to Certain U.S. Courses of Action with Respect to Indochina, 15 June 1954" (approved for release January 2005).

9. Kahin, *Intervention,* 26, 78; Bernard B. Fall, *The Two Vietnams: A Political and Military Analysis*, 2nd revised ed. (New York: Praeger, 1967).

10. U.S. Central Intelligence Agency, *Special National Intelligence Estimate SNIE 63-5-54* (Top Secret), "Post-Geneva Outlook in Indochina, 3 August 1954" (approved for release January 2005).

11. George C. Herring, ed., *The Pentagon Papers*, abridged ed. (New York: McGraw-Hill, 1993), 23-37. Also see Edward Geary Lansdale, *In the Midst of Wars: An American's Mission to Southeast Asia,* 2nd ed. (New York: Fordham University Press, 1991).

12. Ellen J. Hammer, *A Death in November* (Oxford: Oxford University Press, 1987), 52-76.

13. David Halberstam, *The Making of a Quagmire* (New York: Random House, 1964), 147.

14. Neil Sheehan, *A Bright Shining Lie: John Paul Vann and America in Vietnam* (New York: Random House, 1988), Book III.

15. Hammer, *A Death in November*, 284-285.

16. Scott Shane, "Vietnam War Intelligence 'Deliberately Skewed,' Secret Study Says," *New York Times* (December 2, 2005).

17. H. R. McMaster, *Dereliction of Duty: Lyndon Johnson, Robert McNamara, the Joint Chiefs of Staff, and the Lies That Led to Vietnam* (New York: HarperPerennial, 1998).

18. David Maraniss, *They Marched into Sunlight: War and Peace, Vietnam and America, October 1967* (New York: Simon and Schuster, 2003), 345-346.

19. John Prados, *The Hidden History of the Vietnam War* (Chicago: Ivan R. Dee, 1995), 127.

20. C. Michael Hiam, *Who the Hell Are We Fighting? The Story of Sam Adams and the Vietnam Intelligence Wars* (Hanover, NH: Steerforth Press, 2006).

21. U.S. Central Intelligence Agency, *Special National Intelligence Estimate SNIE 14.3-67* (Top Secret): "Capabilities of the Vietnamese Communists for Fighting in South Vietnam, 13 November 1967" (approved for release January 2005).

22. Quoted in Don Oberdorfer, *Tet!* (Garden City, NY: Doubleday, 1971), 105-106.

23. Quoted in Walter Isaacson and Evan Thomas, *The Wise Men: Six Friends and the World They Made* (New York: Touchstone, 1988), 686-687.

24. Telford Taylor, *Nuremberg and Vietnam: An American Tragedy* (Chicago: Quadrangle Books, 1970), 144-145. Also see Richard A. Falk, Gabriel Kolko, and Robert Jay Lifton, eds., *Crimes of War* (New York: Vintage, 1971).

25. See for instance, Vietnam Veterans Against the War, *The Winter Soldier Investigation: An Inquiry into American War Crimes* (Boston: Beacon Press, 1972), 120. In one case, Nathan "Gestapo" Hale, a former Army interrogator from Coatesville, Pennsylvania, produced color slides he had taken of one such interrogation session.

26. James Simon Kunen, *Standard Operating Procedure* (New York: Avon, 1971), 211.

27. Ibid., 80-81.

28. Vietnam Veterans Against the War, *The Winter Soldier Investigation: An Inquiry into American War Crimes* (Boston: Beacon Press, 1972), 104.

29. B. G. Burkett and Glenna Whitley, *Stolen Valor: How the Vietnam Generation Was Robbed of Its Heroes and Its History* (Dallas: Verity Press, 1998); Carleton Sherwood, *Stolen Honor* (Red, White, and Blue Films, 2004).

30. Guenter Lewy, *America in Vietnam* (Oxford: Oxford University Press, 1978).

31. Ibid., 317.

32. John Prados, "Winter Whether," *The New Republic Online* (August 30, 2004), www.newrepublic.com (accessed September 17, 2004).

33. Seymour Hersh broke the story of the My Lai massacre. See his book, *My Lai 4* (New York: Random House, 1970). Also see Richard Hammer, *One Morning in the War* (New York: Coward-McCann, 1970), and Michael Bilton and Kevin Sim, *Four Hours in My Lai* (New York: Viking, 1992).

34. See for example, Neil Sheehan, "Should We Have War Crimes Trials?" *New York Times Book Review* (March 28, 1971); Gary D. Solis, *Son Thang: An American War Crime* (Annapolis, MD: Naval Institute Press, 1997); "Kerry Says His Vietnam Unit Killed Civilians," *Philadelphia Inquirer* (April 26, 2001), 2; Michael Sallah and Mitch Weiss, *Tiger Force* (New York: Little, Brown, 2006); Deborah Nelson and Nick Turse, "A Tortured Past," *Los Angeles Times* (August 20, 2006), www.latimes.com (accessed August 21, 2006).

35. Taylor, *Nuremberg and Vietnam*, 175.

36. See Ronald H. Spector, *After Tet: The Bloodiest Year in Vietnam* (New York: Vintage, 1993).

37. Walter LaFeber, *America, Russia, and the Cold War, 1945–2002*, updated 9th ed. (New York: McGraw-Hill, 2002), 267–276.

38. See, for example, Alfred W. McCoy, *The Politics of Heroin in Southeast Asia* (New York: Harper and Row, 1972).

39. Melvin Small, *Antiwarriors* (Lanham, MD: Scholarly Resources, 2004).

40. Richard A. Gabriel and Paul L. Savage, *Crisis in Command* (New York: Hill and Wang, 1978), 49, 184.

41. Richard Boyle, *Flower of the Dragon* (San Francisco: Ramparts Press, 1972), 222–236.

42. General Bruce Palmer Jr., *The 25-Year War: America's Military Role in Vietnam* (Lexington: University of Kentucky Press, 1984), 155; "Military Discipline: Ebbing Morale of Men at War," *Congressional Quarterly Weekly Report* (February 19, 1972), 391–393; Gabriel and Savage, *Crisis in Command*, 183 (table 3), 202n.

43. Colonel William R. Corson, *The Consequences of Failure* (New York: Norton, 1974), 87; Palmer, *25-Year War*, 155.

44. David Cortright, *Soldiers in Revolt* (Garden City, NJ: Anchor Press, 1975), 6–7.

45. Colonel Robert D. Heinl, "Collapse of the Armed Forces," *Armed Forces and Society* (June 7, 1971).

46. Cortright, *Soldiers in Revolt,* 28.

47. Heinl, "Collapse of the Armed Forces."

48. Lawrence Korb, *The Fall and Rise of the Pentagon* (Westport, CT: Greenwood Press, 1979), 51–52.

49. Melvin Laird, "Iraq: Learning the Lessons of Vietnam," *Foreign Affairs* 84 (November/December 2005), www.foreignaffairs.org (accessed October 19, 2005).

50. Arthur M. Schlesinger Jr., *The Imperial Presidency* (Boston: Mariner Books, 1972/2004), 216, 240, 257–258, 265–269.

51. Ibid., 275.

NOTES FOR CHAPTER 4

1. See, for instance, Townsend Hoopes, *The Limits of Intervention* (New York: David McKay, 1973), and James G. Blight and Janet M. Lang, *The Fog of War: Lessons from the Life of Robert S. McNamara* (Lanham, MD: Rowman and Littlefield, 2005).

2. See Daniel Ellsberg, *Papers on the War* (New York: Simon and Schuster, 1972).

3. See Noam Chomsky, *At War with Asia: Essays on Indochina* (New York: Vintage, 1970).

4. Richard Nixon, *No More Vietnams!* (New York: Arbor House, 1985).

5. See, for example, Colonel Harry G. Summers, Jr., *On Strategy: A Critical Analysis of the Vietnam War* (New York: Dell, 1984).

6. Caspar W. Weinberger, "The Uses of Military Power," *Defense* (January 1985), 2–11.

7. Kenneth J. Campbell, "Once Burned, Twice Cautious: Explaining the Weinberger-Powell Doctrine," *Armed Forces and Society* 24 (Spring 1998): 357–374.

8. John Mueller, *War, Presidents, and Public Opinion* (New York: John Wiley and Sons, 1973).

9. Leslie H. Gelb, "The Essential Domino: American Politics and Vietnam," *Foreign Affairs* (April 1972), www.foreignaffairs.org (accessed August 3, 2006).

10. On the media following, not leading, public opinion on the war, see Stanley Karnow, *Vietnam: A History* (New York: Viking, 1983), 488.

11. Drew Middleton, "U.S. Generals Are Leery of Latin Intervention," *New York Times* (June 21, 1983), A9.

12. Theodore Draper, *A Very Thin Line: The Iran-Contra Affairs* (New York: Hill and Wang, 1991), and Lawrence E. Walsh, *Firewall: The Iran-Contra Conspiracy and Cover-Up* (New York: Norton, 1997).

13. Charles W. Kegley Jr. and Eugene R. Wittkopf, *American Foreign Policy,* 5th ed. (New York: St. Martin's, 1996), 392.

14. David Petraeus, "Military Influence and the Post-Vietnam Use of Force," *Armed Forces and Society* 15 (Summer 1989): 489-505.

15. See Bob Woodward, *The Commanders* (New York: Simon and Schuster, 1991). Also see Lawrence Freedman and Efraim Karsh, *The Gulf Conflict, 1990-1991* (Princeton, NJ: Princeton University Press, 1992).

16. Stephen Budiansky, "Lines in the Sand," *US News and World Report* (October 1, 1990), 30; James Kitfield, *Prodigal Soldiers* (New York: Simon and Schuster, 1995), 13-25.

17. Woodward, *The Commanders,* 324.

18. Ibid., 356.

19. This was confirmed to me in August 1991 in interviews with the faculty of the Department of National Security at the U.S. Army War College at Carlisle Barracks, Pennsylvania; in November 1994 in a lengthy interview with former chair of the Joint Chiefs of Staff, Ambassador William Crowe, at the U.S. Embassy in London; and in a handwritten note to me from General Colin Powell in April 1996.

20. See, for instance, Samantha Power's Pulitzer Prize-winning book, *"A Problem from Hell": America and the Age of Genocide* (New York: Basic Books, 2002).

21. See Kenneth J. Campbell, "Clausewitz and Genocide: Bosnia, Rwanda, and Strategic Failure," *Civil Wars* 1 (Summer 1998): 26-37.

NOTES FOR CHAPTER 5

1. Andrew Bacevich, *The New American Militarism: How Americans Are Seduced by War* (Oxford: Oxford University Press, 2005), 65. Also see John J. Mearsheimer and Stephen M. Walt, "An Unnecessary War," *Foreign Policy* 134 (January/February 2003): 51-59.

2. Michael R. Gordon and General Bernard E. Trainor, *Cobra II: The Inside Story of the Invasion and Occupation of Iraq* (New York: Pantheon Books, 2006), xxxi.

3. Michael Howard, "Constraints on Warfare," in *The Laws of War: Constraints on Warfare in the Western World,* edited by Michael Howard, George J. Andreopoulòs, and Mark R. Shulman (New Haven, CT: Yale University Press, 1994), 2.

4. See Richard A. Falk, Gabriel Kolko, and Robert Jay Lifton, eds., *Crimes of War* (New York: Vintage, 1971); Michael Walzer, *Just and Unjust Wars: A Moral Argument with Historical Illustrations,* 2nd ed. (New York: Basic Books, 1977/1992), 21; and "Nuremberg Judgment," in *Crimes of War: Iraq,*

edited by Richard Falk, Irene Gendzier, and Robert Jay Lifton (New York: Nation Books, 2006), 68.

5. Carl von Clausewitz, *On War* (Princeton, NJ: Princeton University Press, 1976), 88–89.

6. See Richard A. Clarke, *Against All Enemies: Inside America's War on Terror* (New York: Free Press, 2004); James Risen, *State of War: The Secret History of the CIA and the Bush Administration* (New York: Free Press, 2006); John Prados, *Hood-Winked: The Documents That Reveal How Bush Sold Us a War* (New York: New Press, 2004); Mark Danner, *The Secret Way to War: The Downing Street Memo and the Iraq War's Buried History* (New York: New York Review Books, 2006); National Commission on Terrorist Attacks Upon the United States, *The 9/11 Commission Report,* authorized ed. (New York: Norton), 10.3; U.S. Senate Select Committee on Intelligence, "Report on the Postwar Findings about Iraq's WMD Programs and Links to Terrorism and How They Compare with Prewar Assessments," September 8, 2006; U.S. Senate Select Committee on Intelligence, "Report on the Use by the Intelligence Community of Information Provided by the Iraqi National Congress," September 8, 2006.

7. Bacevich, *New American Militarism,* 88; George Packer, *The Assassins' Gate: America in Iraq* (New York: Farrar, Straus & Giroux, 2005), 28; Bob Woodward, *Bush at War* (New York: Simon and Schuster, 2003), 60, 83; John J. Mearsheimer and Stephen J. Walt, "The Israel Lobby," *London Review of Books* 28 (March 23, 2006), www.lrb.co.uk (accessed April 4, 2006).

8. Robert D. Kaplan, *Imperial Grunts: The American Military on the Ground* (New York: Random House, 2005), 5.

9. Ibid., 12.

10. Ibid., 14.

11. Ibid., 5, 14–15.

12. Max Boot, *The Savage Wars of Peace: Small Wars and the Rise of American Power* (New York: Basic Books, 2002), 347.

13. Charles Krauthammer, "The Unipolar Moment," *Foreign Affairs* 70 (America and the World 1990/1991), www.foreignaffairs.org (accessed January 24, 2006).

14. Packer, *Assassins' Gate,* 13, 43; James Mann, *Rise of the Vulcans: The History of Bush's War Cabinet* (New York: Penguin, 2004), 199–200, 212.

15. Project for the New American Century, "Statement of Principles," and "Letter to President Clinton on Iraq, January 26, 1998," www.newamericancentury.org/statementofprinciples (accessed September 16, 2006).

16. Ibid.

17. Ibid.

18. Packer, *Assassins' Gate,* 15: Bacevich, *New American Militarism,* 70.

19. Charles W. Kegley Jr. and Eugene R. Wittkopf, *American Foreign Policy,* 5th ed. (New York: St. Martin's, 1996), 392.

20. Mann, *Rise of the Vulcans,* 125.

21. Packer, *Assassins' Gate,* 26.

22. Bacevich, *New American Militarism,* 27.

23. White House, The National Security Strategy of the United States of America (September 2002), 29, www.whitehouse.gov (accessed April 17, 2003).

24. Clarke, *Against All Enemies,* 30.

25. Woodward, *Bush at War,* 83.

26. Clarke, *Against All Enemies,* 33.

27. Ibid., 267; Packer, *Assassins' Gate,* 61; Risen, *State of War,* 109.

28. Prados, *Hood-Winked,* xii, 175-183, 207-225.

29. Risen, *State of War,* 109; Clarke, *Against All Enemies,* 243.

30. Danner, *Secret Way to War,* 89.

31. Prados, *Hood-Winked,* 350.

32. Clarke, *Against All Enemies,* 268.

33. Thomas E. Ricks, *Fiasco: The American Military Adventure in Iraq* (New York: Penguin Press, 2006), 157.

34. Thomas E. Ricks, "In Iraq, Military Forgot Lessons of Vietnam," *Washington Post,* July 23, 2006, www.washingtonpost.com (accessed July 23, 2006).

35. Anthony H. Cordesman, "Iraq and Foreign Volunteers" (Washington, DC: Center for Strategic and International Studies, November 18, 2005).

36. Leslie H. Gelb, "What to Do in Iraq, a Roundtable: Last Train from Baghdad," *Foreign Affairs* 85 (July/August 2006): 161.

37. David L. Phillips, *Losing Iraq: Inside the Postwar Reconstruction Fiasco* (Boulder, CO: Westview Press, 2005), 57.

38. Larry Diamond, *Squandered Victory: The American Occupation and the Bungled Effort to Bring Democracy to Iraq* (New York: Henry Holt, 2005), 45, 295.

39. *Larry King Live,* May 30, 2005, quoted in Center for American Progress, "Fact or Fantasy: The Administration's Vision of Progress in Iraq," www.americanprogress.org (accessed June 10, 2005).

40. Presidential Address to the American Legislative Exchange Council, August 3, 2005, quoted in Center for American Progress, "Fact or Fantasy."

41. Testimony before the U.S. Senate Foreign Relations Committee, October 19, 2005, quoted in Center for American Progress, "Fact or Fantasy."

42. Ricks, "Military Forgot Lessons."

43. International Crisis Group, "In Their Own Words: Reading the Iraqi Insurgency," Middle East Report # 50 (February 15, 2006), 25-26, www.crisisgroup.org (accessed February 15, 2006).

44. Anthony H. Cordesman, "Losing the War in Iraq?" (Washington, DC: Center for Strategic and International Studies, July 19, 2006).

45. Dana Priest and Mary Jordan, "Iraq at Risk of Civil War, Top Generals Tell Senators," *Washington Post* (August 4, 2006), www.washingtonpost.com (accessed August 4, 2006).

46. David S. Cloud, "No Cutback Likely in U.S. Troop Levels for Iraq Before Spring, Top Regional Commander Says," *New York Times* (September 20, 2006), www.nytimes.com (accessed September 20, 2006).

47. Seymour M. Hersh, "Torture at Abu Ghraib," *New Yorker* (May 10, 2004/posted April 30, 2004), www.newyorker.com (accessed May 6, 2004).

48. U.S. Army, *Article 15-6 Investigation of the 800th Military Police Brigade* (Secret/No Foreign Dissemination), 50.

49. Ibid., 7-8.

50. Seymour M. Hersh, *Chain of Command: The Road from 9/11 to Abu Ghraib* (New York: HarperCollins, 2004), 3-5, 16, 20, 37, 46, 361-367. Also see Mark Danner, *Torture and Truth: America, Abu Ghraib, and the War on Terror* (New York: New York Review Books, 2004).

51. International Committee of the Red Cross, "Iraq: ICRC Explains Position over Detention Report and Treatment of Prisoners" (May 8, 2004), www.icrc.org (accessed May 12, 2004).

52. Human Rights Watch, "Mistreatment of Detainees in U.S. Custody: Letter to President Bush" (May 18, 2004), www.hrw.org (accessed May 18, 2004).

53. Bacevich, *New American Militarism,* 66.

54. Robert F. Worth, "U.S. Military Braces for Flurry of Criminal Cases in Iraq," *New York Times* (July 9, 2006), www.nytimes.com (accessed July 9, 2006).

55. Bob Herbert, "From 'Gook' to 'Raghead,'" *New York Times* (May 2, 2005), www.nytimes.com (accessed May 5, 2005).

56. Ricks, *Fiasco,* 274; Packer, *Assassins' Gate,* 397-398.

57. See Scott Horton, "A Nuremberg Lesson: Torture Scandal Began Far Above 'Rotten Apples,'" Center for Constitutional Rights, "Criminal Indictment against the United States Secretary of Defense Donald Rumsfeld et al.," American Civil Liberties Union and Human Rights First, "The Case against Rumsfeld: Hard Facts Timeline," *In the Name of Democracy: American War Crimes in Iraq and Beyond,* edited by Jeremy Brecher, Jill Cutler, and Brendan Smith (New York: Metropolitan Books, 2005), 112-114, 119-127.

58. From Justice Jackson's Opening Statement, quoted in *Crimes of War: Iraq,* edited by Richard Falk, Irene Gendzier, and Robert Jay Lifton (New York: Nation Books, 2006), 58.

59. Randy Beers, who followed Richard Clarke as counterterrorism expert on the National Security Council, served two tours in Vietnam as a Marine, and lost hearing in one ear from the war, said, "[Karl Rove and the Republicans] ran against Max Cleland saying he wasn't patriotic because he didn't agree 100 percent with Bush on how to do homeland security. Max Cleland, who lost three of his four limbs for this country in Vietnam. I can't work for these people, I'm sorry I just can't." Quoted in Clarke, *Against All Enemies,* 242.

60. Gelb, "What to Do in Iraq: A Roundtable: Last Train from Baghdad," 161.

NOTES FOR CHAPTER 6

1. Dana Priest and Mary Jordan, "Iraq at Risk of Civil War, Top Generals Tell Senators," *Washington Post* (August 4, 2006), www.washingtonpost.com (accessed August 4, 2006).

2. Lawrence J. Korb and Peter Ogden, "Why We Can't Send More Troops," *Washington Post* (September 14, 2006), www.washingtonpost.com (accessed September 19, 2006); Lynn Davis and J. Michael Polich, "Army Stretched Thin: There's No Easy Way out for the Nation," *Rand Review* (Summer 2005), www.rand.org (accessed November 18, 2005); and CNN, "Army Stretched to Breaking Point, Report Says" (January 25, 2006), www.cnn.com (accessed January 25, 2006).

3. Damien Cave, "Army Recruiters Say They Feel Pressure to Bend the Rules," *New York Times* (May 3, 2005), A23.

4. Korb and Ogden, "Why We Can't Send More Troops."

5. Joseph L. Galloway, "Fixing Broken Army Will Take Awhile," *Columbia Daily Tribune* (October 16, 2005), www.showmenews.com (accessed November 5, 2005), and Associated Press, "Murtha Says Army Is Broken" (December 2, 2005), www.military.com (accessed December 12, 2005).

6. Dick Polman, "Public's Support of War Faltering," *Philadelphia Inquirer* (August 14, 2005), www.philly.com (accessed August 14, 2005).

7. PollingReport.com, "Iraq," www.pollingreport.com (accessed March 2, 2006).

8. John Mueller, "The Iraq Syndrome," *Foreign Affairs* 84 (November/December 2005): 44.

9. Robin Toner and Jim Rutenberg, "Partisan Divide on Iraq Exceeds Split on Vietnam," *New York Times* (July 30, 2006), www.nytimes.com (accessed July 29, 2006).

10. Dick Polman, "The Democrats Have No Idea," *Philadelphia Inquirer* (September 24, 2006), C1.

11. Paul D. Eaton, "An Army of One Less," *New York Times* (November 10, 2006), www.nytimes.com (accessed November 10, 2006).

12. Lieutenant General William E. Odom, "Cut and Run? You Bet," *Foreign Policy* 154 (May/June 2006): 61.

13. Larry Diamond, *Squandered Victory: The American Occupation and the Bungled Effort to Bring Democracy to Iraq* (New York: Henry Holt, 2005), 151–152.

14. Leslie H. Gelb, "What to Do in Iraq, a Roundtable: Last Train from Baghdad," *Foreign Affairs* 85 (July/August 2006): 162.

15. Seymour M. Hersh, *Chain of Command: The Road from 9/11 to Abu Ghraib* (New York: HarperCollins, 2004), 365.

16. Odom, "Cut and Run?" 61.

17. Mark Mazzetti, "Spy Agencies Say Iraq War Worsens Terror Threat," *New York Times* (September 24, 2006), www.nytimes.com (accessed September 24, 2006).

18. Quoted in Michael Tomasky, "Against the Neocons," *American Prospect Online* (March 5, 2005), www.prospect.org (accessed July 13, 2005).

19. Bernard Brodie, *War and Politics* (New York: Macmillan, 1973), 1.

20. Martin van Creveld, "Costly Withdrawal Is the Price to Be Paid for a Foolish War," *Forward* (November 25, 2005), www.forward.com (accessed January 25, 2006).

21. Loch K. Johnson, *Seven Sins of American Foreign Policy* (New York: Pearson Longman, 2007), 207-208.

BIBLIOGRAPHY

Adams, Sam. *War of Numbers: An Intelligence Memoir.* South Royalton, VT: Steerforth Press, 1994.

Archer, Michael. *A Patch of Ground: Khe Sanh Remembered.* Central Point, OR: Hellgate Press, 2004.

Associated Press. "Murtha Says Army Is Broken." December 2, 2005. www. military.com (accessed December 12, 2005).

Bacevich, Andrew J. *The New American Militarism: How Americans Are Seduced by War.* Oxford: Oxford University Press, 2005.

Barber, Benjamin R. *Fear's Empire.* New York: Norton, 2004.

Berman, Larry. *Planning a Tragedy.* New York: Norton, 1982.

Biddle, Stephen. "Seeing Baghdad, Thinking Saigon." *Foreign Affairs* 86 (March/April 2006). www.foreignaffairs.org (accessed March 1, 2006).

Bilton, Michael and Kevin Sim. *Four Hours in My Lai.* New York: Viking, 1992.

Blight, James G., and Janet M. Lang. *The Fog of War: Lessons from the Life of Robert S. McNamara.* Lanham, MD: Rowman & Littlefield, 2005.

Boot, Max. *The Savage Wars of Peace: Small Wars and the Rise of American Power.* New York: Basic Books, 2002.

Boyle, Richard. *Flower of the Dragon.* San Francisco: Ramparts Press, 1972.

Brodie, Bernard. *War and Politics.* New York: Macmillan, 1973.

Budiansky, Stephen. "Lines in the Sand." *US News and World Report*, October 1, 1990, 30.

Burkett, B. G., and Glenna Whitley. *Stolen Valor: How the Vietnam Genera-*

tion Was Robbed of Its Heroes and Its History. Dallas, TX: Verity Press, 1998.

Burns, Robert. "Official Probe Supports Allegations in Haditha Killings." *Philadelphia Inquirer*, August 3, 2006. www.philly.com (accessed August 3, 2006).

Campbell, Kenneth J. "Once Burned, Twice Cautious: Explaining the Weinberger-Powell Doctrine." *Armed Forces and Society* 24 (Spring 1998): 357–374.

―――. "Clausewitz and Genocide: Bosnia, Rwanda, and Strategic Failure." *Civil Wars* 1 (Summer 1998): 26–37.

Caputo, Philip. *A Rumor of War.* New York: Owl Books, 1977/1996.

Cave, Damien. "Army Recruiters Say They Felt Pressure to Bend the Rules." *New York Times,* May 3, 2005, A23.

Center for American Progress. "Fact or Fantasy: The Administration's Vision of Progress in Iraq." www.americanprogress.org (accessed June 10, 2005).

Chomsky, Noam. *At War with Asia: Essays on Indochina.* New York: Vintage, 1970.

―――. *Hegemony or Survival: America's Quest for Global Dominance.* New York: Metropolitan Books, 2003.

Churchill, Winston S. *The Second World War,* Volume I: *The Gathering Storm.* New York: Houghton Mifflin, 1948.

Clarke, Richard A. *Against All Enemies: Inside America's War on Terror.* New York: Free Press, 2004.

Clausewitz, Carl von. *On War.* Princeton, NJ: Princeton University Press, 1976.

Cloud, David S. "No Cutback Likely in U.S. Troop Levels for Iraq before Spring, Top Commander Says." *New York Times,* September 20, 2006. www.nytimes.com (accessed September 20, 2006).

CNN. "Hagel: Iraq Growing More Like Vietnam." August 18, 2005. www.cnn.com (accessed August 20, 2005).

―――. "Army Stretched to Breaking Point, Report Says." January 25, 2006. www.cnn.com (accessed January 25, 2006).

Cohen, Richard. "Vietnam's Forgotten Lessons." *Washington Post*, April 11, 2006. www.washingtonpost.com (accessed April 12, 2006).

Cordesman, Anthony H. "Iraq and Foreign Volunteers." Washington, DC: Center for Strategic and International Studies, November 18, 2005.

―――. "Losing the War in Iraq?" Washington, DC: Center for Strategic and International Studies, July 19, 2006. www.csis.org (accessed July 19, 2006).

Corson, Colonel William R. *The Consequences of Failure.* New York: Norton, 1974.

Cortright, David. *Soldiers in Revolt.* Garden City, NJ: Anchor Press, 1975.

Creveld, Martin van. "Costly Withdrawal Is the Price to Be Paid for a Foolish War." *Forward,* November 25, 2005. www.forward.com (accessed January 25, 2006).

Danner, Mark. "The Logic of Force." *New York Review of Books,* June 24, 2004. www.nybooks.com (accessed May 31, 2004).

———. *Torture and Truth: America, Abu Ghraib, and the War on Terror.* New York: New York Review Books, 2004.

———. *The Secret Way to War: The Downing Street Memo and the Iraq War's Buried History.* New York: New York Review Books, 2006.

Davis, Lynn, and J. Michael Polick. "Army Stretched Thin: There's No Easy Way out for the Nation." *Rand Review* (Summer 2005). www.rand.org (accessed November 18, 2005).

Diamond, Larry. *Squandered Victory: The American Occupation and the Bungled Effort to Bring Democracy to Iraq.* New York: Henry Holt, 2005.

———. "What to Do in Iraq, a Roundtable: How to End It." *Foreign Affairs* 85 (July/August 2006): 150-153.

Dobbins, James. "What to Do in Iraq, a Roundtable: No Model War." *Foreign Affairs* 85 (July/August 2006): 153-156.

Dodds, Paisley. "Amnesty Calls Guantánamo Prison 'Gulag of Our Time,' Urges It Be Shut." *Philadelphia Inquirer,* May 26, 2005. www.philly.com (accessed May 26, 2005).

Draper, Theodore. *A Very Thin Line: The Iran-Contra Affairs.* New York: Hill and Wang, 1991.

Durant, Will. *The Story of Civilization,* Volume IV: *The Age of Faith.* New York: Simon and Schuster, 1950.

Eaton, Paul D. "An Army of One Less." *New York Times,* November 10, 2006. www.nytimes.com (accessed November 10, 2006).

Eland, Ivan. *The Empire Has No Clothes.* Oakland, CA: Independent Institute, 2004.

Ellsberg, Daniel. *Papers on the War.* New York: Simon and Schuster, 1972.

———. "The Courage to Talk Withdrawal." June 9, 2005. www.antiwar.com (accessed June 18, 2005).

Falk, Richard A., Irene Gendzier, and Robert Jay Lifton, eds. *Crimes of War: Iraq.* New York: Nation Books, 2006.

Falk, Richard A., Gabriel Kolko, and Robert Jay Lifton, eds. *Crimes of War.* New York: Vintage, 1971.

Fall, Bernard B. *The Two Vietnams: A Political and Military Analysis,* 2nd rev. ed. New York: Praeger, 1968.

Ferguson, Niall. "Empires with Expiration Dates." *Foreign Policy* 156 (September/October 2006): 46-52.

Freedman, Lawrence. "Escalators and Quagmires: Expectations and the Use of Force." *International Affairs* 67, 1 (1991): 15-31.

———. "The Iraq Syndrome: Like McNamara in Vietnam, Rumsfeld Will Leave a Legacy." *Washington Post National Weekly Edition* (January 17-23, 2005), 22-23.

Freedman, Lawrence, and Efraim Karsh. *The Gulf Conflict, 1990-1991.* Princeton, NJ: Princeton University Press, 1992.

Gabriel, Richard A., and Paul L. Savage. *Crisis in Command.* New York: Hill and Wang, 1978.

Galloway, Joseph L. "Fixing Broken Army Will Take Awhile." *Columbia Daily Tribune,* October 16, 2005. www.showmenews.com (accessed November 5, 2005).

Gardner, Lloyd C., and Marilyn B. Young, eds. *The New American Empire.* New York: New Press, 2005.

Gelb, Leslie H. "The Essential Domino: American Politics and Vietnam." *Foreign Affairs* (April 1972). www.foreignaffairs.org (accessed August 3, 2006).

———. "What to Do in Iraq, a Roundtable: Last Train from Baghdad." *Foreign Affairs* 85 (July/August 2006), 160-165.

Gelb, Leslie H., and Richard K. Betts. *The Irony of Vietnam: The System Worked.* Washington, DC: Brookings Institution, 1979.

Gilbert, Martin. *The First World War: A Complete History.* New York: Henry Holt, 2004.

Gordon, Michael R., and General Bernard E. Trainor. *Cobra II: The Inside Story of the Invasion and Occupation of Iraq.* New York: Pantheon Books, 2006.

Halberstam, David. *The Making of a Quagmire.* New York: Random House, 1964.

———. *The Best and the Brightest,* collector's ed. Norwalk, CT: Easton Press, 1969/1988.

Hammer, Ellen J. *The Struggle for Indochina 1940-1955.* Stanford, CA: Stanford University Press, 1955.

———. *A Death in November.* Oxford: Oxford University Press, 1987.

Hammer, Richard. *One Morning in the War.* New York: Coward-McCann, 1970.

Heinl, Colonel Robert D. "Collapse of the Armed Forces." *Armed Forces and Society,* June 7, 1971.

Herbert, Bob. "From 'Gook' to 'Raghead.'" *New York Times,* May 2, 2005. www.nytimes.com (accessed May 5, 2005).

Herring, George C., ed. *The Pentagon Papers,* abridged ed. New York: Mc-Graw-Hill, 1993.

————. *LBJ and Vietnam.* Austin: University of Texas Press, 1994.

————. *America's Longest War,* 4th ed. Boston: McGraw-Hill, 2002.

Hersh, Seymour M. *My Lai 4.* New York: Random House, 1970.

————. "Torture at Abu Ghraib." *New Yorker,* April 30, 2004. www.newyorker.com (accessed May 6, 2004).

————. "The Gray Zone." *New Yorker,* May 24, 2004. www.newyorker.com (accessed May 16, 2004).

————. *Chain of Command: The Road from 9/11 to Abu Ghraib.* New York: HarperCollins, 2004.

————. "The Iran Plans." *New Yorker,* April 17, 2006. www.newyorker.com (accessed April 10, 2006).

Hiam, C. Michael. *Who the Hell Are We Fighting? The Story of Sam Adams and the Vietnam Intelligence Wars.* Hanover, NH: Steerforth Press, 2006.

Hilberg, Raul. *The Destruction of the European Jews.* Chicago: Quadrangle Books, 1961.

Hitchens, Christopher. "Beating a Dead Parrot: Why Iraq and Vietnam Have Nothing Whatsoever in Common." *Slate,* January 31, 2005. slate.msn.com (accessed February 22, 2005).

Hook, Steven W., and John Spanier. *American Foreign Policy Since World War II,* 17th ed. Washington, DC: CQ Press, 2007.

Hoopes, Townsend. *The Limits of Intervention.* New York: David McKay, 1973.

Horton, Scott. "A Nuremberg Lesson: Torture Scandal Began Far above 'Rotten Apples.'" *In the Name of Democracy: American War Crimes in Iraq and Beyond,* edited by Jeremy Brecher, Jill Cutler, and Brendon Smith, 112–114. New York: Metropolitan Books, 2005.

Howard, Michael. "Constraints on Warfare." *The Laws of War: Constraints on Warfare in the Western World,* edited by Michael Howard, George J. Andreopoulos, and Mark R. Shulman, 1–11. New Haven, CT: Yale University Press, 1994.

Human Rights Watch. "Mistreatment of Detainees in U.S. Custody: Letter to President Bush." May 18, 2004. www.hrw.org (accessed May 18, 2004).

International Committee of the Red Cross. "Iraq: ICRC Explains Position over Detention Report and Treatment of Prisoners." May 8, 2004. www.icrc.org (accessed May 12, 2004).

International Crisis Group. "In Their Own Words: Reading the Iraqi Insurgency." Middle East Report No. 50, February 15, 2006. www.crisisgroup.org (accessed February 15, 2006).

Isaacson, Walter, and Evan Thomas. *The Wise Men: Six Friends and the World They Made.* New York: Touchstone, 1988.

Johnson, Loch K. *Seven Sins of American Foreign Policy.* New York: Pearson Longman, 2007.

Kahin, George McTurnan. *Intervention: How America Became Involved in Vietnam.* Garden City, NJ: Anchor, 1987.

Kaplan, Robert D. *Imperial Grunts: The American Military on the Ground.* New York: Random House, 2005.

Karnow, Stanley. *Vietnam: A History.* New York: Viking, 1983.

Kayyem, Juliette. "Engage 'Them.'" *Philadelphia Inquirer,* August 13, 2006. www.philly.com (accessed August 14, 2006).

Kegley, Charles W., Jr., and Eugene R. Wittkopf. *American Foreign Policy*, 5th ed. New York: St. Martin's, 1996.

Kimball, Jeffrey P. *To Reason Why: The Debate about the Causes of U.S. Involvement in the Vietnam War.* Philadelphia, PA: Temple University Press, 1990.

Kitfield, James. *Prodigal Soldiers.* New York: Simon and Schuster, 1995.

Kolko, Gabriel. *The Roots of American Foreign Policy.* Boston: Beacon Press, 1969.

Korb, Lawrence. *The Fall and Rise of the Pentagon.* Westport, CT: Greenwood Press, 1979.

Korb, Lawrence J., and Peter Ogden. "Why We Can't Send More Troops." *Washington Post,* September 14, 2006. www.washingtonpost.com (accessed September 19, 2006).

Krauthammer, Charles. "The Unipolar Moment." *Foreign Affairs* 70 (America and the World 1990/1991). www.foreignaffairs.org (accessed January 24, 2006).

———. "Democratic Doves." *Philadelphia Inquirer,* August 14, 2006. www.philly.com (accessed August 14, 2006).

Kunen, James Simon. *Standard Operating Procedure.* New York: Vintage, 1971.

LaFeber, Walter. *America, Russia, and the Cold War 1945–2002,* updated 9th ed. New York: McGraw-Hill, 2002.

Laird, Melvin. "Iraq: Learning the Lessons of Vietnam." *Foreign Affairs* 84 (November/December 2005). www.foreignaffairs.org (accessed October 19, 2005).

Lansdale, Edward Geary. *In the Midst of Wars: An American's Mission to Southeast Asia*, 2nd ed. New York: Fordham University Press, 1991.

Lewy, Guenter. *America in Vietnam.* New York: Oxford University Press, 1978.

Lowry, Rich. "Bush's Vietnam?" *National Review,* August 15, 2006. www.nationalreview.com (accessed August 22, 2006).

Mann, James. *Rise of the Vulcans: The History of Bush's War Cabinet.* New York: Penguin Books, 2004.

Maraniss, David. *They Marched into Sunlight: War and Peace, Vietnam and America, October 1967.* New York: Simon and Schuster, 2003.

Marrus, Michael R. *The Nuremberg War Crimes Trial 1945–46: A Documentary History.* Boston: Bedford Books, 1997.

Mazzetti, Mark. "Spy Agencies Say Iraq War Worsens Terror Threat." *New York Times,* September 24, 2006. www.nytimes.com (accessed September 24, 2006).

McCoy, Alfred W. *The Politics of Heroin in Southeast Asia.* New York: Harper and Row, 1972.

McGish, Tim. "Collateral Damage or Civilian Massacre in Haditha?" *Time,* March 19, 2006. www.time.com (accessed May 28, 2006).

McMaster, H. R. *Dereliction of Duty: Lyndon Johnson, Robert McNamara, the Joint Chiefs of Staff, and the Lies That Led to Vietnam.* New York: HarperPerennial, 1998.

McNamara, Robert S. *In Retrospect.* New York: Times Books, 1995.

Mearsheimer, John J. *The Tragedy of Great Power Politics.* New York: Norton, 2001.

———. "The Israel Lobby." *London Review of Books* 28 (March 23, 2006). www.lrb.co.uk (accessed April 4, 2006).

Mearsheimer, John J., and Stephen M. Walt. "An Unnecessary War." *Foreign Policy* 134 (January/February 2003): 51–59.

Meyrowitz, Elliott L., and Kenneth J. Campbell. "Vietnam Veterans and War Crimes Hearings." *Give Peace a Chance: Exploring the Vietnam Antiwar Movement*, edited by Melvin Small and William D. Hoover, 129–140. Syracuse, NY: Syracuse University Press, 1992.

Middleton, Drew. "U.S. Generals Are Leery of Latin Intervention." *New York Times*, June 21, 1983, A9.

Mueller, John E. *War, Presidents, and Public Opinion.* New York: John Wiley and Sons, 1973.

———. "The Iraq Syndrome." *Foreign Affairs* 84 (November/December 2005): 44–54.

National Commission on Terrorist Attacks upon the United States. *The 9/11 Commission Report*, authorized ed. New York: Norton.

Nelson, Deborah, and Nick Turse. "A Tortured Past." *Los Angeles Times,* August 20, 2006. www.latimes.com (accessed August 21, 2006).

New York Times (editorial). "The Real Agenda." July 16, 2006. www.nytimes.com (accessed July 16, 2006).

Nicosia, Gerald. *Home to War: A History of the Vietnam Veterans' Movement.* New York: Crown Publishers, 2001.

Nixon, Richard. *No More Vietnams!* New York: Arbor House, 1985.

Oberdorfer, Don. *Tet!* Garden City, NY: Doubleday, 1971.

Odom, William E., Lt. Gen. "Iraq Through the Prism of Vietnam." *Neiman*

Watchdog, March 8, 2006. www.neimanwatchdog.com (accessed March 12, 2006).

———. "Cut and Run? You Bet." *Foreign Policy* 154 (May/June 2006): 60–61.

Olson, James S., and Randy Roberts. *Where the Domino Fell: America and Vietnam 1945–2004,* 4th ed. Maplecrest, NY: Brandywine Press, 2004.

Packer, George. *The Assassins' Gate: America in Iraq.* New York: Farrar, Straus & Giroux, 2005.

Palmer, General Bruce Jr. 1984. *The 25-Year War: America's Military Role in Vietnam.* Lexington: University of Kentucky Press.

Petraeus, David. "Military Influence and the Post-Vietnam Use of Force." *Armed Forces and Society* 15 (Summer 1989): 489–505.

Philadelphia Inquirer. "Kerry Says His Vietnam Unit Killed Civilians." (April 26, 2001): 2.

Phillips, David L. *Losing Iraq: Inside the Postwar Reconstruction Fiasco.* Boulder, CO: Westview Press, 2005.

Podhoretz, Norman. *Why We Were in Vietnam.* New York: Simon and Schuster, 1982.

PollingReport.com. "Iraq." www.pollingreport.com (accessed March 2, 2006).

Polman, Dick. "Public's Support for War Faltering." *Philadelphia Inquirer,* August 14, 2005. www.philly.com (accessed August 14, 2005).

———. "The Democrats Have No Idea." *Philadelphia Inquirer,* September 24, 2006, C1, C5.

Powell, Colin L. *My American Journey.* New York: Random House, 1995.

Power, Samantha. *A Problem from Hell: America and the Age of Genocide.* New York: Basic Books, 2002.

Prados, John. *The Hidden History of the Vietnam War.* Chicago: Ivan R. Dee, 1995.

———. *Hood-Winked: The Documents That Reveal How Bush Sold Us a War.* New York: New Press, 2004.

———. "Winter Whether." The New Republic Online, www.newrepublic.com (accessed September 17, 2004).

Priest, Dana, and Mary Jordan. "Iraq at Risk of Civil War, Top Generals Tell Senators." *Washington Post,* August 4, 2006. www.washingtonpost.com (accessed August 4, 2006).

Project for the New American Century. "Statement of Principles" and "Letter to President Clinton on Iraq, January 26, 1998." www.newamericancentury.org (accessed September 16, 2006).

Record, Jeffrey, and W. Andrew Terrill. *Iraq and Vietnam: Differences, Similarities, and Insights.* Carlisle Barracks, PA: U.S. Army War College, May 2004.

Reisman, W. Michael, and Chris T. Antoniou, eds. *The Laws of War: A Comprehensive Collection of Primary Documents on International Law Governing Armed Conflict.* New York: Vintage Books, 1994.

Ricks, Thomas E. *Fiasco: The American Military Adventure in Iraq.* New York: Penguin Press, 2006.

———. "In Iraq, Military Forgot Lessons of Vietnam." *Washington Post,* July 23, 2006. www.washingtonpost.com (accessed July 23, 2006).

Risen, James. *State of War: The Secret History of the CIA and the Bush Administration.* New York: Free Press, 2006.

Sallah, Michael, and Mitch Weiss. *Tiger Force.* New York: Little, Brown, 2006.

Schabas, William. *Genocide in International Law.* Cambridge: Cambridge University Press, 2000.

Schlesinger, Arthur M., Jr. *The Imperial Presidency.* Boston: Mariner Books, 1973/2004.

Shane, Scott. "Vietnam War Intelligence 'Deliberately Skewed,' Secret Study Says." *New York Times,* December 2, 2005. www.commondreams.org (accessed July 31, 2006).

Sheehan, Neil. "Should We Have War Crimes Trials?" *New York Times Book Review,* March 28, 1971.

———. *A Bright Shining Lie: John Paul Vann and America in Vietnam.* New York: Random House, 1988.

Sherwood, Carleton. *Stolen Honor.* Red, White, and Blue Films, 2004.

Small, Melvin. *Antiwarriors.* Lanham, MD: Scholarly Resources, 2004.

Solis, Gary D. *Son Thang: An American War Crime.* Annapolis, MD: Naval Institute Press, 1997.

Spector, Ronald H. *After Tet.* New York: Vintage, 1993.

Summers, Harry G., Jr. *On Strategy: A Critical Analysis of the Vietnam War.* New York: Dell, 1984.

Taylor, Telford. *Nuremberg and Vietnam: An American Tragedy.* Chicago: Quadrangle Books, 1970.

Tomasky, Michael. "Against the Neocons." *American Prospect Online,* March 5, 2005. www.prospect.org (accessed July 13, 2005).

Toner, Robin, and Jim Rutenberg. "Parties Divide on Iraq Exceeds Split on Vietnam." *New York Times,* July 30, 2006. www.nytimes.com (accessed July 29, 2006).

Tucker, Robert W., and David C. Hendrickson. *The Imperial Temptation: The New World Order and America's Purpose.* New York: Council on Foreign Relations Press, 1992.

Turse, Nick, and Deborah Nelson. "Civilian Killings Went Unpunished." *Los Angeles Times,* August 6, 2006. www.latimes.com (accessed August 6, 2006).

U.S. Army. *Article 15-6 Investigation of the 800th Military Police Brigade* (Secret/No Foreign Dissemination).

Vietnam Veterans Against the War. *The Winter Soldier Investigation: An Inquiry into American War Crimes.* Boston: Beacon Press, 1972.

Walsh, Lawrence E. *Firewall: The Iran-Contra Conspiracy and Cover-Up.* New York: Norton, 1997.

Walt, Stephen M. *Taming American Power.* New York: Norton, 2005.

Walzer, Michael. *Just and Unjust Wars: A Moral Argument with Historical Illustrations*, 2nd ed. New York: Basic Books, 1977/1992.

Weinberger, Caspar W. "The Uses of Military Power." *Defense* (January 1985): 2-11.

Western, Jon. "The War over Iraq: Selling the War to the American Public." *Security Studies* 14 (January–March 2005): 99-130.

Westmoreland, William C. *A Soldier Reports.* Garden City, NY: Doubleday, 1976.

White House. The National Security Strategy of the United States of America. September 2002. www.whitehouse.gov (accessed April 17, 2003).

Winterfilm Collective. *Winter Soldier.* Millarium Zero, 1972/2005.

Woodward, Bob. *The Commanders.* New York: Simon and Schuster, 1991.

———. *Bush at War.* New York: Simon and Schuster, 2003.

———. *Plan of Attack.* New York: Simon and Schuster, 2004.

Worth, Robert F. "U.S. Military Braces for Flurry of Criminal Cases in Iraq." *New York Times,* July 9, 2006. www.nytimes.com (accessed July 9, 2006).

INDEX

123

Freedom, 56, 77
Friendly fire, 30, 31, 34
FTA Show, The, 54
Fukuyama, Francis: strategic vision of, 78
Fundamentalist Islam, spread of, 5

Gates, Robert, 93
Gelb, Leslie, 96; on public opinion, 67
Geneva Accords (1954), 43
Geneva Conventions (1949), 86; class on, 18, 19; neocons and, 78; violation of, 49
Genocide, x, 3, 9, 71
Gentili, Alberico, 73
Going native, 21
Grunts, 16, 20, 35; fragging by, 53
Guantánamo Prison, 86
Guerrillas, 27, 32, 44, 47
Guerrilla war, 34, 82
Gulf of Tonkin "incidents," 45
Gulf War, Weinberger Doctrine and, 69, 70

Habeas corpus, selective suspension of, 76
Haditha, slaughter at, 87
Hagel, Chuck, 6, 79, 95
Halberstam, David, 8, 44
Hale, Nathan "Gestapo," 104n25
Hamilton, Lee, 95
Hammer, Ellen, 42, 45
Headquarters Company, Hill 689 and, 22
Heinl, Robert: on military breakdown, 54
Hersh, Seymour, 95, 96; Abu Ghraib and, 85–86; My Lai massacre and, 105n33
Hezbollah, Marine barracks bombing by, 69

Hill 689: battle at, 22–23; photo of, 22
Hill 881, 22
Hitchens, Christopher, 3
Ho Chi Minh, 3, 41, 42, 43
Hoi An, 26
Holbrooke, Richard: Viet-malia syndrome and, 71
Holocaust, 9
Homeland security, 110n59
Hoover, J. Edgar, 15
Hope, Bob, 54
"Hot" areas, 24, 25
House Select Committee on Intelligence, 64
Howard, Michael: on just war, 73–74
Hue, 20
Humanitarian assistance, 71
Human rights, 71, 87
Human Rights First, 87
Human Rights Watch, letter of protest by, 86–87
Humiliation, xii, 1, 68, 69
Hussein, Saddam, xi; al-Qaeda and, 75, 80, 81; atrocities by, 3; neocons and, 78; removing, 79; September 11th and, 75, 80; WMDs and, 80, 81

I Corps, xv, 19
Idealism, language of, 77
Imperial Congress, 65
Imperial Grunts: The American Military on the Ground (Kaplan), 75
Imperialism, 5, 75–76
Imperial policing, 76–77
Imperial presidency, 56, 98; checks on, 64, 65, 68
Imperial strategy, 76, 78
Institutional prevention, 64–66
Insurgency, 83; beginning of, 82;

and, 97; rapid, 55, 93, 94, 95, 96,
97; responsibility for, 94
WMDs. *See* Weapons of mass
destruction
Wolfowitz, Paul: Defense Planning
Guide and, 77; deferments for, 79;
September 11th and, 80; strategic
vision of, 78
Woodward, Bob, 70, 80
World War I: lessons from, 9;
quagmire metaphor and, 8

World War II: casualties in, 67;
compelling purpose for, 67; dad
and, 11; as just struggle, x; lessons
from, 10; public support for, 67
W-PD. *See* Weinberger-Powell
Doctrine
WPR. *See* War Powers Resolution
WSI. *See* Winter Soldier Investigation

Zinni, Anthony, 95
Zogby poll, 97

About the Author

Kenneth J. Campbell is associate professor of political science and international relations and director of the International Relations Program at the University of Delaware. He served with the Marines in Vietnam and later joined the Vietnam Veterans Against the War. Campbell earned all of his degrees from Temple University. His previous book was *Genocide and the Global Village* (Palgrave, 2001). Campbell is married, has a grown daughter, and lives in Philadelphia, where he listens to Italian opera, watches old movies, and plays golf badly.